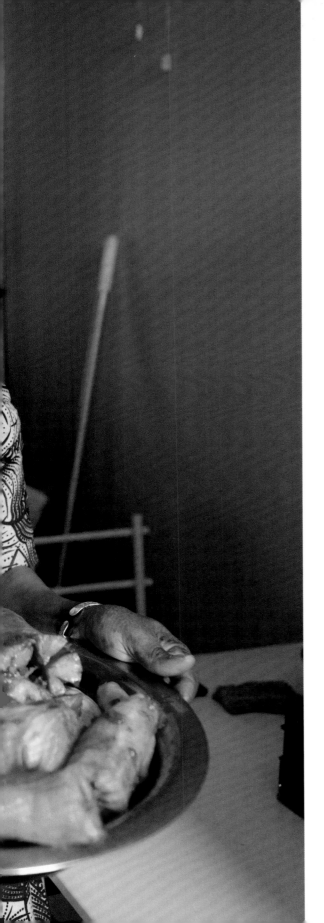

*Left: Friends Bintou
Coulibaly (left) and Fatima
Abbas prepare spicy West
African Rice with Fish and
Vegetables (page 90) for
a family meal. Page viii:
Burgundy-Style Beef Braised
in Red Wine (page 116), as
served at the classic bistro
Joséphine Chez Dumonet.
Page ix: an apartment
building on Paris's Left Bank.*

Contents

*Opposite: The first course of
the Allegra family's Easter
meal is served in a home in
Paris's northern suburbs.*

5 - 6 - 2017
PAVÉ POLOGNE
HACHÉ FRANCE
TÊTE FRANCE
HAMPE FRANCE
21

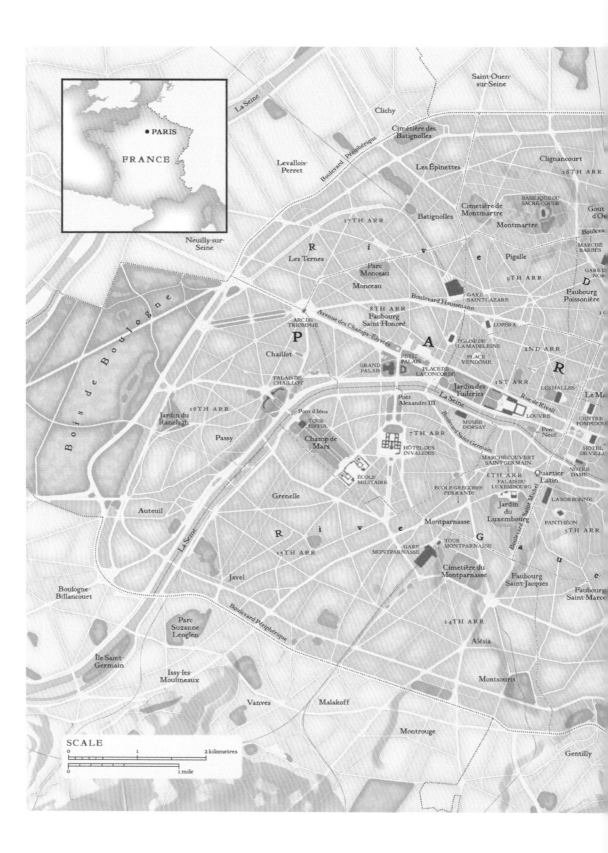

The Enlightened City

Situated on a lowland of islands and sandbanks at an arc of the river Seine, the city of Paris has been a place of civic importance since 259 BC, when a Celtic tribe called the Parisii began trading goods on its shores. On the southern (known as the Left) bank, conquering Romans built elaborate theaters, temples, and forums, establishing a hub of commerce and education with a lavish aesthetic; it was known as Lutetia. After marshland to its north was filled in, the city's cultural center began to shift to the northern (known as the Right) bank; its first municipal government was seated there, with its roots in an organization that oversaw the city's bustling river trade. By the late 12th century—several dynasties, social upheavals, and insurrections later—Paris, as it had come to be known, was the apex of political, economic, religious, and artistic life in what would become France. The metropolis is renowned for its architectural marvels, from the Arc de Triomphe to Notre Dame, and the dozens of ornate bridges that span the Seine. Still, its more than 400 parks weave the natural world into daily life; the Bois de Boulogne alone covers 2,090 pastoral acres. The economic powerhouse of the nation, it is the most ethnically diverse city in Europe; most immigrants hail from Portugal, Spain, and the former French colonies of Morocco and Algeria. Since the Revolution, the city has been divided into twenty subdivisions called arrondissements, which spiral clockwise from the center like a snail's shell.

CITY POPULATION *2,148,271*
METROPOLITAN POPULATION *10,958,000*
OLDEST BRIDGE *Pont Neuf, construction begun in 1578*
NUMBER OF BOTTLES OF WINE CONSUMED ANNUALLY *697 million*
NUMBER OF PEOPLE ATTENDING OPERA, BALLET, AND CONCERTS ANNUALLY *800,000*
OLDEST FOOD MARKET *Marché des Enfants Rouges, founded in 1678*
PATRON SAINT *Geneviève, often portrayed holding bread*

A casual approach to cooking makes an old-fashioned kitchen like Bénédict Beaugé's a pleasure to cook in.

Picnicking on summer evenings alongside the Canal Saint-Martin is a popular Paris tradition.

1

The City of Savoir Vivre

Introduction

Opposite: Diane Reungsorn's recipe for French Shepherd's Pie (page 133) has a dash of oyster sauce, a savory innovation of her own. Page xxii: Roast Veal with Shallot Gravy (page 119).

I t is a rain-slicked spring evening in Paris's fifteenth arrondissement. Dusk has begun to fall as Frédéric Ramade, a film director in his fifties, walks by a crowded bistro. Through its steamy windows, a waiter can be seen taking bread in a cloth-lined basket to a table. Ramade too is carrying bread; a baguette is tucked under his arm. It's one of two gifts he is bringing his friend, the art director and cookbook author Bénédict Beaugé. In Ramade's backpack is a bottle of wine he hopes will pair well with what Beaugé plans to serve for dinner.

In his flat on Rue de Lourmel, Beaugé hears the knock on his door and smiles: his invitation specified eight o'clock, and it's twenty minutes after. It is an unwritten rule in Paris that dinner guests should allow their hosts a bit of extra time to make sure everything is in order. Beaugé quickly checks that all of the appetizers are in place. Yes. There on his cutting board, beside a stack of books, are a bowl of garlic-and-lemon-spiked green olives from an excellent Moroccan shop in the Belleville neighborhood and cold, thick slices of the ham known as *jambon de Paris*. In his seventies, Beaugé might appreciate his guest offering a hand, but he still has the energy and passion to tend to everything here, from the bowl of freshly made mayonnaise to the vase of pink peonies on the kitchen counter.

Welcomed in, Ramade accepts a warm kiss on the cheek and a glass of wine from Beaugé. It's a ten-year-old Pinot Noir, just the thing for dispelling the evening chill. "Oh, my goodness," murmurs Ramade at the table as he bites into the first course, meaty spears of tender blanched asparagus to be dipped in the mayonnaise. Beaugé insists the credit goes not to him but to the season. Asparagus, the men agree, is one of the real triumphs of spring.

Ramade and Beaugé are food obsessives. Anywhere else in the world they might be thought of as extreme. But their interest in pursuing excellence in the things they cook and eat is something that virtually everyone in this city shares in one way or another. Their first meeting was in the 1990s at one of Beaugé's legendary *déjeuners du dimanche* (Sunday lunches). These affairs started out for close friends (and whomever those friends might be having a fling with at the time), but eventually, scores of people began showing up, with Beaugé cooking every dish single-handedly in his modestly sized kitchen. "Do I remember correctly," Ramade asks, eyes sparkling behind his glasses, "that during one of your lunches that famous cross-dressing coloratura really stood on your coffee table and sang?"

Beaugé laughs at the memory. "Yes, between the soup and the coq au vin, I believe." Mostly what he remembers, though, is what a mad dash it was to get every plate to the table at optimal temperature. But this is why so many Parisian three-star chefs, from Alain Passard to the late, great Joël Robuchon, have proudly

called Beaugé their friend: When it comes to French cooking, especially of the traditional variety, Beaugé is a guru.

It's time for the main course. Beaugé opens the oven door, releasing the scent of roast veal and caramelized shallots. In a cast-iron casserole on the table sits a gratin of new potatoes baked with cream, one of his specialties. All of the dishes are spare, but Beaugé's commitment to cooking them exactly as he was taught by his mother and grandmothers yields impeccable results.

He uncorks the bottle Ramade brought, and sets out a crock of Dijon mustard. Rain patters against the window. "A roast in cold weather makes you feel so comfy," says Beaugé as he spoons pan gravy over the veal, his concentration unbroken. "Don't you think?"

The French idiom *savoir vivre* means having an intelligent approach to enjoying life, greeting each situation with refinement and poise. Parisian meal preparation is an example of this concept. To cook the dishes in this book is to embody this attention to detail, to tap into the wealth of knowledge that the French have accumulated over centuries of careful practice in their kitchens. And so,

when you prepare these recipes, take time to observe the particulars, from attentively selecting the right variety of butter and being vigilant about continuously and gently stirring the beurre blanc sauce to prevent it from breaking to the position of the plates you place on the table. Follow these steps and you begin to understand what distinguishes the remarkable cuisine of Paris.

Even a dish as easy to prepare as roast lamb studded with garlic and rosemary will demonstrate the advantages of French technique. Endeavoring to make somewhat more complex recipes, such as classic quiche Lorraine, a custard of eggs, cream, and bacon in a golden, buttery *pâte brisée* tart shell, will be rewarded. With practice, you might discover the thrill of making your own puff pastry, a sublimely flaky dough used in three recipes in this book: pastry cups stuffed with mushrooms and chicken in béchamel sauce, a savory pastry topped with salt-packed anchovies and onion marmalade, and a strawberry dessert with vanilla custard. Whether it means choosing only the freshest-looking bundles of herbs with which to make stuffed garden tomatoes, or considering what wine would fortify your guests to go back out into a misty spring night, the Parisian way is a truly civil approach to dining.

*Above: Botanique chef
Sugio Yamaguchi displays
a just-made pâté en croûte.
Opposite: The elegant
dining room of Botanique
Restaurant in the eleventh
arrondissement.*

The Pont d'Iéna spanning the Seine, with the Eiffel Tower in the background, on a fall afternoon.

"Paris always ends up feeding you."

—ALFRED CAPUS, FRENCH JOURNALIST AND PLAYWRIGHT, 1858 TO 1922

2

Small Dishes, Grand Flavors

Appetizers

I n a building that dates back to the 1600s, on a street so narrow that cars can barely squeeze through, a Friday night gathering is about to get underway in the apartment of Nicole Knaus and her husband, Antoine Philippe. The young professional couple—she is a teacher, he is a lawyer—have had a demanding workweek, and they've been looking forward to unwinding with friends.

An ordinary *apéro* is an array of small and toothsome snacks served before a meal. An *apéro dînatoire*, which Knaus and Philippe are hosting tonight, is one of the most charming of Paris's culinary traditions: it allows a host to serve a banquet without necessarily having to cook, thereby giving the host time to mingle. To attend an *apéro dînatoire* is to gather for an evening of good cheeses, small plates, charcuterie, and wine. It might be supplemented by a homemade dish or two, though a host can also purchase the whole affair.

The first guests to arrive, straight out of the crowded *métro*, have a sense of anticipation as they mount the creaking spiral staircase to their destination. The passageways of the old building are dark, with rustic walls of stucco and aging timber. "It's like Rapunzel's tower," Philippe's mother, Pascale, remarks.

"But we will be fed so much better than Rapunzel was," jokes her friend, Victoria Ross, a professional cook from New Zealand.

Inside the apartment, the windows are open to the summer evening and the patchwork of rooftops below. Across the street, the centuries-old church is so close you can almost touch it. Beyond that, the lights of the city sparkle. The sensory experience a host creates is a key aspect of a successful *apéro dînatoire*, and to that end, music plays at just the right tempo and volume for relaxing. When the guests arrive, Knaus is busy putting out a plate of meltingly soft and creamy reblochon cheese and, fresh out of the oven, a platter full of sweet, slow-roasted cherry tomatoes flavored with thyme and rosemary. It's a dish that usually gets devoured within moments of her setting it on the table.

Soon the apartment is full of the sounds of people talking, debating, laughing, eating, and enjoying. Philippe acts as greeter and sommelier, pouring wine for his mother and Champagne for Ross. Welcoming Sanford McCoy, a documentary filmmaker who lives in Pantin, on the outskirts of Paris, Philippe says, "Thank you again for dinner last week. I haven't been able to stop thinking about your first course."

Knaus overhears him. "Yes, that terrine," she agrees. "We were tempted to steal the leftovers to take home."

McCoy laughs and says, "I had a plan to bring the rest of it on a picnic this weekend. But, well, I ended up eating it all."

Cream of Asparagus Soup (page 36) is a traditional herald of spring and a starter of simple elegance.

"My grandmother's Sunday lunches would last from noon until 10 p.m. As I child, I was spellbound by them. I thought they would keep going on forever."

—FRÉDÉRIC RAMADE, FILM DIRECTOR

An *apéro dînatoire* is an alternative to a sit-down meal. If a standard multi-course dinner is in store, however, the Parisian home cook is sure to serve an appetizer that is in harmony with what is to follow. For instance, it might be a warm lentil salad, cooked with lardons (matchsticks of bacon) and herbs, allowed to cool slightly, and dressed with a walnut oil vinaigrette. The dish feels substantial, yet there's a lightness to it that awakens the palate without overwhelming it.

Another appetizer that is both rich and sprightly is country-style Pork Terrine, made with pork and pork liver that have been marinated in white wine, onion, and bay leaves for a complex savoriness. Served cool and eaten with a dab of Dijon mustard, cornichons (tartly flavored small French pickles), and a good baguette, few starters can match it. As it is easy and gratifying to prepare, many Parisian home cooks make their own rather than buying it from a butcher. Duck Confit Salad with Asparagus is an appetizer made of confit, a preparation of duck braised in its own fat until it is a tender marvel. Although duck confit, or *confit de canard*, is generally eaten warm (and on the bone), in this recipe, it is served at room temperature, finely minced and mixed with chives and then adorned with spears of white and green asparagus. It is as spectacular to look at as it is delicious.

Soup, too, has a significant role to play at the home table, as a traditional meal almost invariably begins with a soup course. If the main dish is going to be something considerable, such as a roast, consider preparing a cream of asparagus soup, a relatively simple recipe that is nevertheless an exemplar of its kind. It is a delicate distillation of the fresh flavor of asparagus. An appetizer like this soup, or any of the offerings at a good *apéro dînatoire*, is more than a starter: it is a friendly welcome to the table.

Frédéric Ramade presents his guests with Puff Pastry Cups with Chicken and Mushrooms (page 35), or "queen's little bites," as his grandmother used to during her own Sunday lunches in Alsace.

The Art of the Apéro

An *apéro* is a thoughtful assembly of hors d'oeuvres and small dishes composed mostly of quality store-bought foods. A successful one is all about balance: a spread might include rich, cured foods, typically charcuterie, such as dried sausages and earthy-tasting country pâté, that contrast with brighter-tasting ones like olives, crudités (raw vegetables), blanched asparagus, or sardines drizzled with lemon juice. Cheeses, too, are chosen with a range in mind: mild Morbier, for example, will be served with its polar opposite, funky ripe Roquefort. And of course, there are always baguettes for eating with everything. From this alluring range of tastes and textures, guests can create whatever combinations they like. An *apéro* doesn't have to be an extravagant affair, however: you can make a pared-down one just for yourself, to relish at the end of a long workday, or for a small gathering of friends. By purchasing a few more substantial items, you can expand a basic get-together into an *apéro dînatoire*, which is a full supper of small bites. Whether you intend to serve just snacks or enough food to constitute a meal, consider your purchases carefully. What is the best of what's available? What pairs well with what? Give some thought to what you pour, too—wine, Champagne, or cocktails—for the finest *apéro* you can present. (For a wine-buying guide, see page 79.)

A trusty wooden cutting board serves as both a cooking implement and a serving tray for the elements of an apéro.

Tomme de Savoie

Epoisse

Chêvre

Fleischkäse
(Swiss-style pâté)

Paris-style smoked ham

Cornichons

Saucisson sec de
porc (French-style
pork sausage)

Baguette

Fresh Herb and
Lemon Zest Dip
(page 36)

Garlic-lemon
olives

Crudités

Butter

Landjäger (Swiss-style
pork and beef sausage)

Sardines

Comté

Roquefort

Spiced olives

Roasted
Cherry
Tomatoes
with Herbs
(page 36)

Le Pouligny Saint Pierre

Ossau Iraty

Oven-roasted wild asparagus

Olives—enjoyed in apéros, cooked dishes, and on their own—come in all sorts of tempting shapes, sizes, and flavors at a stall in the Marché Barbès.

Tunisian Salad (page 39),
a true Paris classic, employs
some of the pronounced, spicy
flavors of North Africa, like
preserved lemon and harissa.

"Why is French cheese so excellent? It's a result of all sorts of things, including responsible animal husbandry, excellent raw milk, and our country's ancient traditional cheesemaking techniques. But what really makes our cheese the best in the world is our cheesemakers and their passion. They are the real heroes of French cheese."

—LAURENT DUBOIS, PROPRIETOR OF FROMAGERIE LAURENT DUBOIS

Joanna Dos Santos, an employee at Fromagerie Laurent Dubois, one of Paris's most highly regarded cheese shops, holds three varieties of goat cheese.

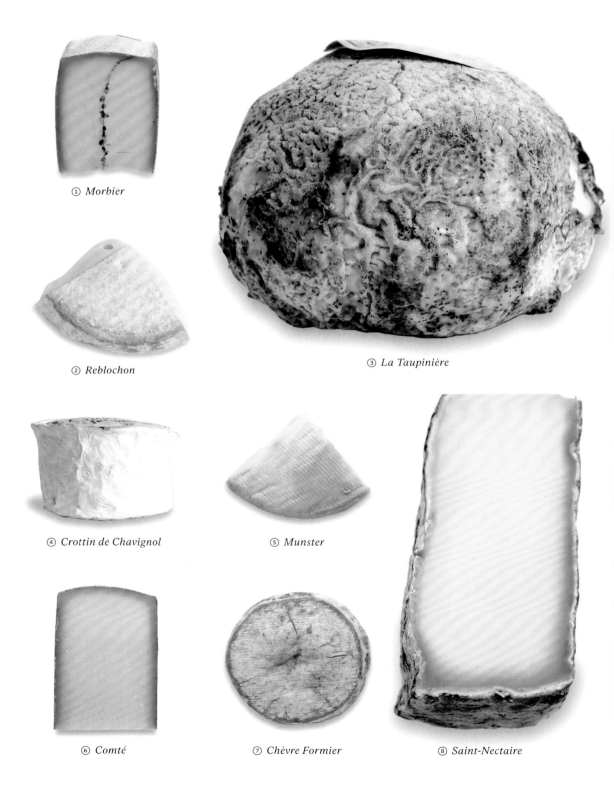

① *Morbier*

② *Reblochon*

③ *La Taupinière*

④ *Crottin de Chavignol*

⑤ *Munster*

⑥ *Comté*

⑦ *Chèvre Formier*

⑧ *Saint-Nectaire*

⑨ *Camembert*

⑩ *Chaource Fermier*

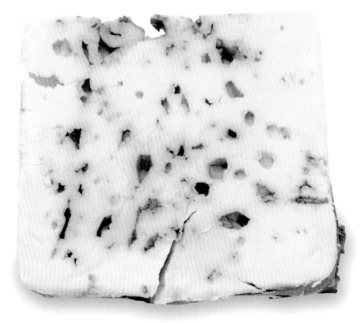

⑪ *Roquefort*

⑬ *Époisses*

⑫ *Charolais*

⑭ *Bethmale*

Sampling the World's Finest Cheese

The French adore their cheese: it is a staple food, a component of a proper *apéro*, and features in meals as its own course before dessert. France produces the world's greatest cheeses in more than a thousand regionally made varieties; of these, a limited number have been granted *appellation d'origine contrôlée* (AOC) status, a certification based on terroir, the environmental characteristics that make a product unique to its place of origin. France exports many of its cheeses, and what follows is a sample of the types available in North America. **Morbier** ① With a distinctive center line of vegetable ash, this is a slightly tangy semisoft cow's milk cheese. **Reblochon** ② This wonderfully oozy, intense cheese pairs well with nuts. **La Taupinière** ③ Sheathed in blue-gray mold, this aromatic goat's milk cheese is creamy, smooth, and snappy-sweet. **Crottin de Chavignol** ④ A goat's milk cheese with a rippled rind, this cheese is creamy and nutty when young, as shown. **Munster** ⑤ This mild-tasting washed-rind Alsatian cheese (also shown opposite) pairs well with beer. **Comté** ⑥ A superior melting cheese that has a crystallized texture and aromas of pan-browned butter and roasted nuts. **Chèvre**

Fermier ⑦ This catchall name is used for small-batch fresh goat's milk cheeses, which typically have a smooth texture and a slightly sharp farmyard taste. **Saint-Nectaire** ⑧ Made in the Auvergne, this silky-textured cheese boasts flavors of hay and mushroom and has a toothsome edible rind. **Camembert** ⑨ A widely available cow's milk cheese with a rich, buttery flavor, Camembert, made in Normandy, has a runny interior and a delicious rind. **Chaource Fermier** ⑩ Soft and a little bit crumbly, this cow's milk cheese has a milky, salty flavor. **Roquefort** ⑪ Moist, rich, and sharp, with a creamy-crumbly texture, blue-veined Roquefort is made from sheep's milk. **Charolais** ⑫ Produced in Burgundy, this is a smooth-textured, subtle-tasting mix of cow's milk and goat's milk. **Époisses** ⑬ This pungent cow's milk cheese has a spicy, salty flavor and a creamy texture. **Bethmale** ⑭ A product of the Pyrenees, this is a mild, semisoft cow's milk cheese with a barnyard aroma.

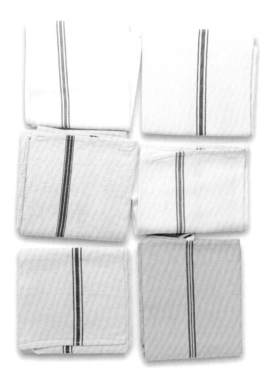

Useful Beauty

For centuries, the *torchon*, France's best-loved type of kitchen towel, has been prized for its utility, durability, and good looks. Made of linen, a textile derived from flax fibers, the *torchon* is strong and absorbent and dries faster than its cotton counterpart. Since the finest linen has always come from the flax fields of Normandy, a region in France's northwest, it's not surprising that even the humble kitchen towel would attain the height of elegance in both form and function. In the past, most French homes had a storehouse of *torchons* at hand: thin ones for drying and polishing glassware and heavier weights for harder jobs. For much of the nineteenth century, they were unadorned, but over time, they gained the distinctive red stripes that still embellish them today. There are theories as to why red is the near-ubiquitous color for this decoration; inexpensive dye and its ability to withstand bleaching are among the theories. The history behind the design of the stripe itself, however, remains intriguingly obscure. Antique handmade *torchons* are still sold at flea markets and online, but contemporary reproductions work just as well, and the modern Parisian home and professional kitchen always have at least a few at the ready.

Duck Confit Salad with Asparagus
Salade de Confit de Canard aux Asperges

In this recipe, based on one from Parisian Pascal Decary, minced duck confit and chives are topped with green and white asparagus spears and dressed in a simple but elegant vinaigrette (see photograph, page 6). Note that if you make your own duck confit, you must begin the cooking process a few days ahead of time. For information on the difference between green and white asparagus, see page 196.

Serves 4

> About 20 thick green and/or white asparagus
>   spears, woody ends discarded
> 2 homemade (page 118) or store-bought duck legs
>   confit with skin, boned and finely chopped
> 1 tablespoon finely minced fresh chives
> 1 tablespoon walnut or extra-virgin olive oil
> 1 teaspoon red or white wine vinegar
> Freshly ground black pepper
> Baguette, for serving

1 You may need to peel the asparagus spears, as the outside can be quite fibrous. Fill a large, wide saucepan or large skillet half full with salted water and bring to a boil over high heat. Add the asparagus and cook until the bottoms are just tender when pierced with a fork, about 5 minutes. Drain into a colander and set aside.

2 In a medium bowl, mix together the duck and chives. Transfer to a serving platter. In another medium bowl, whisk together the oil and vinegar. Add the asparagus and turn to coat evenly with the vinaigrette.

3 Arrange the asparagus spears atop the confit mixture in a sunburst pattern, alternating green and white spears if using two varieties. Drizzle any vinaigrette remaining in the bowl over the top. Finish with a few grinds of pepper; salt is unnecessary, as the confit provides sufficient saltiness. Serve with the baguette.

Puff Pastry Cups with Chicken and Mushrooms

Bouchées à la Reine

The phrase *bouchées à la reine*—"queen's little bites"—is an apt description for these individual puff pastry cups and filled with poached chicken, sautéed mushrooms, and béchamel sauce. This recipe (see photograph, page 12) is adapted from one belonging to Frédéric Ramade. You'll get the best result using homemade puff pastry, but store-bought puff pastry will do.

Makes 12 small filled pastries

PASTRY CUPS

Half-batch French Puff Pastry (page 194) or 1¼ pounds thawed store-bought all-butter puff pastry, such as Dufour (see page 193)

1 egg yolk, lightly beaten

FILLING

6 ounces boneless, skinless chicken breast (about half a small breast)

1 cup Béchamel Sauce (page 196)

1 tablespoon unsalted butter

⅓ small yellow onion, minced

1½ cups button mushrooms (about 6 ounces), finely chopped

⅓ cup sherry or white wine

Salt and freshly ground black pepper

1 Preheat the oven to 375°F. If using store-bought pastry, unfold the sheets gently to avoid cracking (if the pastry is not pliable, let it sit for a few more minutes at room temperature). Place the dough—homemade or store-bought—on a lightly floured work surface and sprinkle a little flour on top of it. Gently roll into a rectangle about 13 by 10 inches and about ⅓ inch thick. Work swiftly so the dough doesn't warm up.

2 Using a fluted round cutter 3 inches in diameter, cut out twelve pastry rounds. Transfer the rounds to a sheet pan, spacing them about 1½ inches apart. To form the top for each pastry cup, center a smooth-sided round cutter 2 inches in diameter in the center of each pastry round and carefully press down, stopping just short of cutting through the bottom of the round. Lightly brush the tops and sides of each round with the egg yolk.

3 Bake the pastry cups until puffed and golden, 35 to 40 minutes. Transfer to a wire rack until cool enough to handle. Then, using a paring knife, gently cut around the smaller round in the top of each pastry and pry it up with the tip of the knife, taking care not to break it. As each small round is removed, set it aside on the wire rack. (These smaller rounds will be used as lids for the finished pastries.) Using your index finger, press down gently on the center of each large round to form a cup shape. Set the cups and lids aside to cool.

4 To make the filling, in a medium saucepan, combine the chicken and lightly salted water to cover and bring to a simmer over medium-low heat. Cook just until the chicken is opaque at the center when tested with a knife tip, about 10 minutes. Drain the chicken, transfer to a plate, and let cool, then cut into ¼-inch cubes. Prepare the béchamel sauce and set it aside.

5 In a 12-inch skillet, melt the butter over medium heat. Add the onion and cook, stirring frequently, until translucent but not golden, about 4 minutes. Add the mushrooms and cook, stirring often, until thoroughly softened, about 10 minutes. Add the sherry and chicken, season with a generous pinch of salt and a good grind of pepper, and continue to cook, stirring often, until about half of the liquid has evaporated, about 2 minutes. Transfer the filling to a medium bowl. Add the béchamel and mix well. Taste for salt and add more if necessary. Preheat the oven once again to 375°F.

6 To assemble each pastry, spoon about 2 tablespoons of the filling into a pastry cup, slightly overfilling it, and top with a lid, placing it slightly ajar. Arrange the filled pastries on a sheet pan and bake for about 5 minutes to warm them through and allow the flavors to meld. Transfer to a serving dish and serve warm.

Cream of Asparagus Soup

Velouté d'Asperges

Inspired by a recipe from Parisian artist and home cook Yves Koerkel, this version of a classic appetizer soup made with asparagus (see photograph, page 17) is hearty yet refined. White asparagus, called for here, has a fleeting season, but no worries, as this soup is just as delicious made with the green variety—or even another vegetable, such as broccoli.

Serves 4

3 tablespoons unsalted butter
1 yellow onion, finely chopped
1½ tablespoons all-purpose flour
1 pound thick white or green asparagus, woody ends discarded and spears cut crosswise into 3-inch lengths (about 3 cups)
1 medium russet potato, peeled and cut into rough 2-inch cubes (about 1 cup)
4 cups French Chicken Broth (page 188)
1 cup whole milk
Salt and freshly ground black pepper
1 tablespoon minced fresh flat-leaf parsley leaves, for serving

1 In a large saucepan, melt the butter over medium heat, tilting the pan in a circular motion as it melts. Add the onion and cook, stirring often, until just translucent, about 4 minutes. Add the flour, stir to mix well, and cook, stirring constantly, until the flour is sticky and lightly golden, about 2 minutes. Add the asparagus, potato, broth, milk, and ½ teaspoon salt and stir to mix well, making sure the flour is fully incorporated. Cover partially and cook, stirring occasionally, until the asparagus and potato are fork-tender, about 20 minutes.

2 Remove from the heat and let cool slightly. Working in batches, add the contents of the pan to a blender and puree until the vegetables are pulverized but not smoothly ground; the soup should have subtle texture. Taste for salt and adjust the seasoning if needed. Ladle into bowls, top each serving with a grind or two of pepper and a little parsley, and serve immediately.

Fresh Herb and Lemon Zest Dip

Dip aux Fines Herbes

A plate of raw vegetables accompanied by a dip nearly always makes an appearance at an *apéro*. This bright-tasting dip (see photograph, page 22), based on one from Victoria Ross and made with crème fraîche (Greek yogurt is a good substitute), lemon zest, and a farmers' market's worth of minced herbs, is also excellent on a sandwich in lieu of mayonnaise. For the vegetables, consider serving a combination of cauliflower florets, carrot sticks, French breakfast radishes, and cherry tomatoes.

Makes about 1½ cups

1½ cups crème fraîche (see page 191) or plain whole-milk Greek yogurt
1 teaspoon Dijon mustard
3 tablespoons minced fresh chives
3 tablespoons minced fresh tarragon
3 tablespoons minced fresh flat-leaf parsley
1 teaspoon finely grated lemon zest
Hearty pinch of cayenne pepper
Salt and freshly ground black pepper

1 In a medium bowl, combine the crème fraîche, mustard, chives, tarragon, parsley, lemon zest, and cayenne, and mix well. Season with ½ teaspoon salt and a couple of grinds of pepper. Taste and adjust the seasoning with salt and pepper if needed.

2 Serve right away, or cover and refrigerate for up to a few hours before serving.

Roasted Cherry Tomatoes with Herbs

Tomates à la Nicole

In roasting, these tomatoes (see photograph, page 23) blister and release their juices, gaining a texture that's almost like a *confiture* (jam)—perfect for dipping into with a crunchy baguette. This recipe is inspired by one from Nicole Knauss and works best if you start with tomatoes that are sweet tasting.

Warm Lentil Salad (page 39).

Serves 4

- 4 cups stemmed cherry tomatoes (about 1⅓ pounds)
- 2 garlic cloves, well bruised
- 3 tablespoons extra-virgin olive oil
- 4 fresh or dried thyme sprigs, or ½ teaspoon dried thyme leaves
- 2 fresh rosemary sprigs, or 1 teaspoon dried rosemary needles
- Salt and freshly ground black pepper

1 Preheat the oven to 275°F. In an 8-inch square or round baking dish, combine the tomatoes, garlic, oil, thyme, rosemary, ¾ teaspoon salt, and a pinch of pepper and stir to mix well.

2 Roast the tomatoes, stirring regularly to prevent scorching, until lightly golden and beginning to burst open, about 50 minutes. Taste and adjust the seasoning with salt if needed. Serve at once or allow to cool slightly.

Tunisian Salad

Salade Tunisienne

This salad (see photograph, page 27) is a popular appetizer in the Tunisian restaurants of Paris. The fresh flavors of cucumber and tomato take on complexity from the addition of tuna, olives, preserved lemon, and dried mint. A dab of the North African salsa-like condiment harissa, made from chiles, provides smoky heat. This recipe makes enough salad for one, but it can be easily scaled up. Halved hard-boiled eggs make it more substantive.

Serves 1

- ¾ cup diced English cucumber
- 1 small Roma tomato, diced
- ¼ medium yellow onion, diced
- 1 teaspoon dried mint leaves, finely crumbled
- 6 pit-in sun-dried black olives or small, pit-in cracked green olives (such as Picholine)
- 2 tablespoons extra-virgin olive oil
- Salt and freshly ground black pepper

Country-Style Pork Terrine (page 42), as served at Joséphine Chez Dumonet, garnished with Little Gem lettuce and a roast garlic clove.

- One 5-ounce jar or can olive oil–packed tuna, drained
- 1 thick slice North African–Preserved Lemon (page 195) or store-bought preserved lemon, rinsed, quartered, then sliced (optional)
- 2 teaspoons harissa (see page 192; optional)
- Baguette, for serving

1 In a medium bowl, combine the cucumber, tomato, onion, mint, olives, oil, ¼ teaspoon salt, and a couple of grinds of pepper. Toss the mixture, then taste for salt and pepper, adding more if needed. Spoon the mixture onto an individual serving plate.

2 Arrange the tuna on top of the mixture and put the lemon pieces and harissa (if using) on the side. Toss again before serving, if you like. Serve with the bread.

Warm Lentil Salad

Salade de Lentilles

In this salad (see photograph, page 37), bacon lends the already earthy taste of lentils an additional savor. It is a terrific dish to have in your everyday repertoire, as it is equally good as a first course, a side dish, a picnic food, or even an easy light meal with good bread.

Serves 4

- 1½ cups Le Puy lentils (see page 192) or small green lentils, rinsed
- 5 ounces slab bacon, cut into lardons 2 inches long and ¼ inch wide and thick (about 1 cup)
- 2 fresh or dried thyme sprigs, or a generous pinch dried thyme leaves
- 2 bay leaves
- Salt
- ⅓ cup walnut, grapeseed, or olive oil
- 1 tablespoon red wine vinegar
- 1 teaspoon Dijon mustard
- Freshly ground black pepper
- 4 large pieces leaf lettuce
- ½ cup minced fresh flat-leaf parsley
- About 5 small shallots, halved lengthwise then sliced crosswise ¼ inch thick (about ½ cup)

Remembrance of Things Past

Les Halles, the main centrally located fresh-food market of Paris, was, from its inception in the early 1100s, a mecca for the city's food lovers. In Émile Zola's 1873 novel *Le Ventre de Paris* (*The Belly of Paris*), he describes the market as it was in his time: a place of prosperity and pleasure, housed in a masterwork of fin de siècle architecture, with ten soaring arched pavilions, or *halles* (halls), each dedicated to a gastronomic specialty and its sellers—a constellation of shellfish vendors in one, cheesemongers in another, and so on. (The photo, above, shows a portion of the market in the early 1960s.) One could, as Julia Child wrote in the 1950s, "find virtually anything under the sun there." By the late 1960s, Les Halles was in need of enormous repairs, but the government elected instead to demolish the historic site, dismantling its beautiful pavilions and relocating the wholesale market to a suburb south of the capital and calling it Rungis. Decades (and billions of euros) later, the updated and expanded Les Halles, now a shopping mall and transportation hub, cannot be said to have a much of a soul. The original and legendary market lives on only in the history books, in the memories of older Parisians, and in anyone who had the good fortune to experience shopping in its splendid vaulted arcades.

1 In a medium saucepan, combine the lentils, bacon, thyme, bay leaves, ½ teaspoon salt, and water to cover by 1 to 2 inches. Bring to a boil over high heat, turn down the heat to medium-low, and simmer, uncovered and stirring occasionally, until the lentils are just tender, 30 to 45 minutes; the timing depends on the lentil variety used. Take care to add water if the lentils begin to dry out.

2 Just before the lentils are ready, make the vinaigrette and dress the lettuce. In a bowl, whisk together the oil, vinegar, mustard, a good pinch of salt, and a few grinds of pepper. In another bowl, lightly dress the lettuce with a few teaspoons of the vinaigrette and set aside. Reserve the remaining vinaigrette for dressing the lentils.

3 Drain the lentils and remove and discard the thyme sprigs and bay leaves. Transfer to a serving bowl and stir in the parsley, shallots, and a few grinds of pepper. Add the reserved vinaigrette and stir to mix well. Taste and adjust the seasoning with salt and pepper if needed.

4 Divide the still-warm lentils among four plates and put a piece of dressed lettuce alongside each serving. Serve immediately.

Country-Style Pork Terrine
Terrine de Campagne

A good terrine or pâté (a more refined, less coarse version of a terrine) is part of a respectable *apéro*. Many regional variations exist, but this rustic and subtle version strikes the perfect balance of meat and flavorings. To make it, you'll need pork leg, pork liver, and unprocessed pork or beef fat (not lard), which means visiting a butcher, and you'll need to begin putting it together a couple of days in advance of serving. Serve the terrine with Dijon mustard and cornichons or with vinaigrette-dressed Little Gem or baby romaine lettuce as shown in the photograph on page 38—and don't forget plenty of good, crusty baguette to spread it onto.

Makes one 8½ by 4½-inch terrine

1 pound boneless pork leg, cut into
    2-inch chunks

About 5 ounces pork liver, cut into
    2-inch chunks

½ medium yellow onion, halved

4 bay leaves

1 cup dry white wine (such as Chardonnay)

10 ounces pork or beef fat, cut into
    2-inch chunks

2 eggs

3 garlic cloves, finely minced

1 teaspoon ground ginger

½ teaspoon ground cloves

Salt and fresh coarse-grind black pepper

1 Two days before serving, in a medium non-reactive bowl, combine the pork leg, pork liver, onion, bay leaves, and wine. Mix well, cover, and refrigerate overnight.

2 The next day, preheat the oven to 350°F. Remove and discard the onion and bay leaves, then transfer the meats and marinade into a fine-mesh sieve set over a bowl. Reserve ½ cup of the marinade and discard the remainder. Using a meat grinder fitted with the coarse plate or a food processor, grind or pulse the pork leg, pork liver, and fat until you have a coarse paste; some small chunks of meat add desirable roughness.

3 In a large bowl, combine the ground meats and fat with the eggs, garlic, ginger, cloves, 1½ to 2 teaspoons salt, 2 teaspoons pepper, and ¼ cup of the reserved marinade. Mix together all of the ingredients until evenly distributed and the eggs are fully incorporated. The mixture will be quite wet and loose—it should slip through your fingers. If the texture is drier than this description, add as much of the remaining ¼ cup marinade as needed, a tablespoon at a time, to achieve the correct consistency.

4 Transfer the meat mixture to a mold: either an 8½ by 4½-inch bread loaf pan or a 1-quart pâté terrine (see page 189). It will shrink slightly as it bakes. Cover tightly with aluminum foil or the pâté terrine's lid, place the mold into a roasting pan, and add water to the roasting pan to reach about halfway up the sides of the mold. Bake until the center of the terrine is cooked through and no red juice emerges when it is punctured with a thin skewer or a fork, about 1 hour 40 minutes. It is ready when an instant-read thermometer inserted into the center registers 155°F.

5 Remove the terrine from the oven and set aside atop a plate to cool for 30 minutes. Select something that's heavy enough to compress the terrine but malleable enough to fit into the pan, and lay it on top of the foil. (You can improvise; a bag of sugar or beans placed inside another plastic bag is a good option.) If you're using a pâté terrine and it's equipped with a weight, place the weight on top of the terrine. Let the terrine sit for 2 hours. Then remove the weight and refrigerate the terrine, covered, overnight.

6 The following day, remove the foil or lid and run a knife around the edges of the terrine to loosen it from the mold. Flip the mold upside down onto a serving platter and serve.

3

From Market to Table, with Love

Vegetables

*Above: Poached Spring
Vegetables with Lemongrass-
Dill Dressing (page 64) is
a pure celebration of the
season. Opposite: lush
chestnut trees in the Jardin
du Luxembourg. Page 44:
New Potatoes Baked in
Cream (page 64).*

Catherine Barnouin presents an heirloom recipe: spinach tart cooked in a flaky pâte brisée *crust (page 65).*

White asparagus has a fleeting season, but it is well worth seeking out for its delicate flavor and eye-catching appeal.

Catherine Barnouin, a public relations professional who has lived in Paris off and on for more than four decades, arrives at the street market that occurs every Saturday morning in her Left Bank neighborhood. Her canvas tote bag slung over her shoulders, she makes her way along the rows of stalls. She's greeted with a wink and a thumbs-up from her favorite fruit vendor, for she cuts a stylish figure, with thoughtful blue eyes set off by her silvery-blond hair.

It might have been quicker to go to the chain supermarket just down the street. But an astute shopper buys what is seasonal, not what is merely available, and Barnouin is nothing if not astute. Why should she (or anyone, for that matter) expend energy trying to make, say, a pale-pink imported tomato taste good when the vendors' tables at this market are heavy with locally grown, freshly picked vegetables? Beets, fava beans, new potatoes, escarole, chicory, arugula, zucchini, and more are within reach. Barnouin watches a dapper gentleman carefully place his purchase of carrots into a string bag and she decides to take his good example, as the carrots on offer are slender and crisp, bound to be sweet. A bundle of them goes into her own bag along with a basket of blackberries.

The French tend to base cooking decisions partly on what is available to them, partly on the mood and climate of the day. Now, with a sense of summer having finally settled in, a special childhood memory is coming into Barnouin's mind: her grandmother used to spend summertime in the Alpine village of Barcolette, and one of the dishes she would serve the family whenever the grandchildren came to visit was local-style spinach tart cooked in a *pâte brisée* crust. Traditionally made with foraged wild greens, the tart is spiked with bacon and enriched with béchamel sauce. It's just the kind of meal the children would have been served on a summer evening in the mountains back then. There's a vendor here who always has the freshest, most irresistibly tender spinach. And there he is, his distinctive handwoven haji cap making him easy to spot. Barnouin buys two kilos' worth.

A tart like the one Barnouin will make is quite rich, so a side salad would, she reflects, be just the right companion. Now all that's left for her to do is decide which lettuce is best. Today's lettuces are all appealing in different ways. There are piles of small, crunchy Sucrine heads next to gorgeous Rougette de Montpellier, splayed open the width of two outstretched hands and with red-tinged leaves. With a discerning eye, she selects a *laitue verte*, similar to what in the United States is called butter or Boston lettuce, with tender leaves and a tightly packed center. She also picks out a pert bundle of chives.

No sooner does Barnouin arrive back at her spacious loft apartment—located in the

Parisian Carrot Vinaigrette (page 67) retains its crunch, making it a staple of Paris picnic spreads.

Provençal-Style Braised Artichokes (page 68) is a classic of the southern French countryside that is now an everyday Parisian dish.

building where the modern master painter Yves Klein once had his studio—than her cell phone rings. She works for the tourism communications department for the city of Paris, and every day there is a lot to juggle, even on weekends. She empties the spinach into a large colander and returns the most important call first, putting the phone on speaker mode. By the time she's done organizing a meeting with a visiting journalist, she has washed all of the spinach and poured herself a glass of crisp rosé to sip while she cooks.

Drying her hands on a white linen tea towel with a classic red stripe—Barnouin has a weakness for pretty linens—she turns to her maternal grandmother's old kitchen notebook, where the recipes are written in cursive. It's one of her treasured keepsakes, and not just for sentimental reasons. She still draws a lot of inspiration from these excellent old recipes.

As she nibbles the last bite of golden crust, Barnouin reflects that lunch was as good as she'd hoped. Better yet, her son called and they had some time to catch up—it was as if she'd conjured family togetherness by cooking her grandmother's dish. Now, with a feeling of contentment, Barnouin wraps the leftover tart for tomorrow's dinner and gives thought to her salad course.

Like many Parisians, she often likes to combine two or more types of greens in the same salad, mixing bitter ones, such as dandelion, arugula, or watercress, with sweeter lettuces. But for this meal, she's sticking to her original idea of something basic and refreshing.

She washes the *laitue verte* leaves one by one and dries them with a clean towel, to avoid bruising them in a salad spinner. Then she rubs the interior of her trusty wooden salad bowl with a peeled bruised garlic clove. Next, she prepares a vinaigrette directly in the bowl: a drizzle of fruity olive oil, a splash of red wine vinegar, a dab of Dijon mustard, salt, and freshly ground pepper, all whisked until a vinaigrette as smooth and thick as honey forms. After adding the lettuce, she snips in a generous quantity of the chives. Their sharp fragrance marries those long-ago summer evenings in the mountains to the present.

Absolute Freshness

Choose a lettuce variety that complements your meal, or mix it with stronger-flavored shoots and greens—and tie it all together with a vinaigrette (see the recipe below). **Roquette** ① (arugula, opposite) has a refreshing spiciness and bitterness. **Feuilles de betterave** ② (young beet greens) are wholesome and have a mineral flavor. **Cresson** ③ (watercress) has a crisp edible stem and small clover-size leaves that taste sharply peppery. **Laitue verte** ④ is similar to butter or Boston lettuce, tender and mild. **Sucrine** ⑤, known in the United States as Little Gem lettuce, resembles a baby romaine, with sweet, tightly packed, crunchy leaves. **Feuille de Chêne** ⑥ (oak leaf) is a delicate variety with red-tinged leaves. **Rougette de Montpellier** ⑦ is as visually stunning as it is delicious. **Batavia** ⑧ (green leaf) is sturdy, reliable, and tastes of a summer field.

Classic Vinaigrette

The traditional ratio for French vinaigrette is three or more parts oil to one part vinegar. Extra-virgin olive oil is common, or consider grapeseed, safflower, or sunflower. Add wine vinegar (see page 197, or substitute fresh lemon juice), a bit of Dijon mustard (about ½ teaspoon for every 3 tablespoons oil), and salt and freshly ground black pepper to taste and whisk until fully emulsified. Toss your salad just before serving.

Glorious Chaos

The Marché Barbès, shown at left, with its atmosphere of an old-world bazaar, is a boisterous and colorful part of Paris's public market system, possibly its busiest as well as its most affordable. Held beneath the elevated *métro* tracks along the Boulevard de la Chapelle in the Goutte d'Or neighborhood, the market is open Wednesday and Saturday mornings, and a wise shopper arrives early. Its sole, many-blocks-long thoroughfare is jammed with an incredible array of West African, North African, and Middle Eastern vendors. At either end are stalls selling jewelry, clothing, shoes, and trinkets, but in the center is a profusion of edible goods: fresh seafood, roast chicken, mounds of parsley and mint, *merguez* sausages, North African–style phyllo pastries, almond-stuffed date sweets direct from Yemen, piles of lemons and fresh spinach, cheeses, olives, bread, and a miscellany of uncategorizable items, everything at low cost. The thundering clatter of the passing trains overhead mingles with the full-throated cries of stallholders hawking their wares and prices. And all along this narrow artery, a river of jostling customers vie for the best prices and the freshest provisions.

"There are two main ways I prepare vegetables. The first involves lots of meticulous steps, it's the professional way. I honestly don't follow that method very often. The second is the home method. I love to slowly stew vegetables and coax out their essence. I also love to roast them—roots and squashes especially—and serve them with a vinaigrette and a handful of chopped fresh herbs scattered on top. It's simple but it is French food at its best."

—BÉNÉDICT BEAUGÉ, ART DIRECTOR AND COOKBOOK AUTHOR

Above: The Marché Bastille,
a street market in the
eleventh arrondissement,
provides endless inspiration
to the people who shop there.
Opposite: Sautéed Turnips
with Cinnamon (page 68).

New Potatoes Baked in Cream

Gratin Dauphinois

The delicate golden crust that forms on the potatoes is a little piece of heaven. This dish (see photograph, page 44) makes an excellent vegetarian main course too.

Serves 4 to 6

> 1 cup water
> 1 cup whole milk
> 2 pounds medium new or waxy white
>   potatoes, peeled and sliced crosswise
>   a little less than ¼ inch thick
> 1 garlic clove
> Salt and freshly ground black pepper
> ⅛ teaspoon freshly grated nutmeg
> ¾ cup heavy cream

1 Preheat the oven to 350°F. In a 4-quart saucepan, combine the water and milk and bring to a boil over high heat. Add the potatoes and garlic. Reduce the heat to medium-high and cook at a rolling boil, stirring frequently, until you can just pierce the potatoes with a fork, about 5 minutes. Using a slotted spoon, transfer the potato slices to a plate. Discard the garlic, leaving the cooking liquid in the pan.

2 Butter a 2-quart gratin dish or a 7 by 11-inch baking pan. Arrange the potatoes in the prepared dish, layering them in neat rows and overlapping the slices slightly. Evenly season with 1¼ teaspoons salt, a few grinds of pepper, and the nutmeg. Pour the water-milk cooking liquid over the potatoes; the liquid should come about three-fourths of the way up the sides of the dish. Discard any remaining liquid.

3 Bake until the potatoes are almost tender and nearly all of the liquid has been absorbed, 1 hour to 1 hour 20 minutes. Pour the cream evenly over the potatoes and bake until their surface is golden brown, about 35 minutes. Serve at once.

Poached Spring Vegetables with Lemongrass-Dill Dressing

Estouffade Printanière

Based on a time-honored dish that showcases an array of spring vegetables poached only briefly before they are dressed, this recipe (see photograph, page 47), inspired by chef Sugio Yamaguchi, is a chic revision incorporating an intriguing dressing made of lemongrass, ginger, dill, cilantro, and lime.

Serves 4

> About 3 tablespoons unsalted butter,
>   or as needed
> 1 stalk lemongrass, bottom 3 inches only
>   (tough outer layers discarded), cut into
>   thin crosswise pieces
> 1-inch piece fresh ginger, peeled and thinly
>   sliced against the grain
> 2 tablespoons fresh cilantro leaves
> 2 tablespoons fresh dill leaves
> ½ small lime with skin intact, seeded and
>   coarsely chopped
> 2 tablespoons extra-virgin olive oil
> Salt
> ½ cup water
> 2 cups small new potatoes (no more than 1 inch
>   or so in diameter), peeled
> 1 cup small white spring onions (bulbs only)
>   or pearl onions, outer layer discarded
> 25 haricots verts (see page 197) or young green
>   beans, stems and tails trimmed, cut into
>   2-inch lengths (about 2 cups)
> 1½ cups trimmed and cut-up asparagus
>   (the thinnest you can find), in 2-inch lengths
> 2 cups broccoli florets, in 2-inch florets
> ½ cup shucked fresh fava beans (see page 197)
> 2 tablespoons torn fresh peppermint
>   or spearmint leaves
> 2 tablespoons small fresh basil leaves,
>   or torn larger basil leaves
> Freshly ground white or black pepper

1 Preheat the oven to its lowest setting and place an ovenproof dish in the oven. Bring a medium saucepan filled halfway with salted water to a steady, rolling boil and add 1 table-spoon of the butter. While the water is heating, make the dressing. In a blender, combine the lemongrass, ginger, cilantro, dill, lime, oil, a generous pinch of salt, and the water. Blend until well ground, then taste for salt, adding more if needed. Strain through a fine-mesh sieve into a small bowl.

2 When the water is boiling, move quickly, cooking each type of vegetable in a separate batch. As you work, add more salt, butter and/ or hot water as needed to maintain the original level, and always have the water at a rolling boil before adding the next batch of vegetables. The potatoes, onions, green beans, asparagus, broccoli, and, lastly, fava beans should be cooked until tender but still slightly crisp. When they're ready, remove each batch of vegetables from the water with a slotted spoon, and trans-fer them to the ovenproof dish to keep warm while you cook the rest—except for the fava beans, which should be transferred to a col-ander and held under cold running water until cool enough to handle, then gently squeezed until each bean is free from its skin.

3 Transfer the warm vegetables to a serving bowl, add the dressing, mint, and basil, and mix gently. Taste and add salt if needed. Garnish with pepper and serve immediately.

Catherine's Old-Fashioned Spinach Tart

Tarte aux Épinards

Spinach in béchamel sauce fills this tradi-tional vegetable tart (see photograph, page 49). Because it can be served hot or at room tem-perature, it would be equally welcome at a Sunday brunch, in a picnic basket, or on the dinner table. Omit the bacon to make it a vege-tarian main dish.

Serves 5

> 1 batch Flaky Tart Pastry (page 194)
> 2½ cups Béchamel Sauce (page 196)
> 2 pounds fresh spinach leaves, or 1 pound frozen spinach, thawed
> 7 ounces slab bacon, cut into ¼-inch cubes (about 1½ cups)
> Freshly ground white or black pepper and salt (optional)
> All-purpose flour, for the work surface
> 2 egg yolks, beaten

1 Have ready the pastry dough and béchamel sauce. If using fresh spinach, wash it thoroughly, then transfer it, still wet, to a large pot. Place over medium heat, cover, and cook, stirring occasionally, until it has wilted but is still bright green, about 4 minutes. Pour into a colander. When it's cool enough to handle, squeeze out as much of the liquid as possible, then chop it coarsely. If using frozen spinach, squeeze out as much of the liquid as possible and chop coarsely.

2 In a skillet, cook the bacon over medium heat, stirring occasionally, until just golden, about 4 minutes. Transfer it to a large bowl. Add the spinach and béchamel sauce to the bowl and mix well. Add pepper to taste and stir to com-bine. Taste for seasoning, adding a pinch or two of salt if necessary.

3 Fifteen minutes before baking, remove the two dough disks from the refrigerator, unwrap, and dust each lightly with flour. Preheat the oven to 375°F. Have ready a 9½-inch pie plate. On a lightly floured work surface, roll out one disk, working from the center outward and rotating it clockwise a quarter turn after every few passes, until you have a circle about 13½ inches in diam-eter and ⅛ to ¼ inch thick. If the dough sticks to the rolling pin, dust the dough with a tiny bit more flour. To lift the pastry easily into the pie plate, place the plate next to it. Set the rolling pin in the center of the round, fold half of the dough over it, and then lift the rolling pin to place the dough onto the plate. Gently press the dough into the bottom and up the sides of the plate

(there will be overhanging pastry). Prick the bottom about twenty times with the tines of a fork. Pour the spinach mixture into the pastry-lined pie plate. Roll out the second disk using the same method. Lift the dough round and carefully slide it over the filling. Using scissors, trim the overhang to 1 inch. Fold the 1-inch overhang under itself to create a high lip and crimp the edge with your fingers or with the tines of a fork. Use the scissors to clip a few rows of small vents in the top crust. Brush the top crust and the edges with the egg yolks. Bake until the crust is evenly golden brown, about 1 hour 10 minutes. Let cool slightly on a wire rack and serve hot, or let cool and serve at room temperature.

Parisian Carrot Vinaigrette
Carottes Râpées

This tangy salad (see photograph, page 53) of thin strips of carrot dressed with a lemony vinaigrette is a favorite for an outdoor meal or a cocktail party. Use young carrots with a lot of snap and sweetness.

Serves 4

    2 tablespoons fresh lemon juice
    ½ teaspoon Dijon mustard
    3 tablespoons extra-virgin olive oil
    Salt and freshly ground black pepper
    1 pound carrots, peeled and cut into very fine
        3-inch-long julienne strips
    1 tablespoon finely minced fresh flat-leaf parsley
        leaves, plus more for garnish

In a small bowl, whisk together the lemon juice and mustard. Then, whisking continuously, slowly add the oil until fully incorporated. Whisk in ½ teaspoon salt and ¼ teaspoon pepper. In a medium bowl, combine the carrots and parsley, pour the vinaigrette over them, and mix well. Taste and add more salt if needed. Garnish with a bit more parsley.

Nouvelle Ratatouille

Nouvelle Ratatouille
Ratatouille à la Botanique

In this ratatouille (see photograph, opposite), based on one served at Botanique Restaurant, the vegetables are diced and presented atop thick slices of eggplant.

Serves 4

    1¼ pounds small or medium stem-on eggplants,
        cut into lengthwise halves (if small) or
        ½-inch-thick lengthwise slices (if medium)
    Salt
    3 tablespoons extra-virgin olive oil, plus more
        if needed
    1 medium yellow onion, cut into ¼-inch cubes
        (about 1 cup)
    2 garlic cloves, bruised
    5 fresh or dried thyme sprigs, or ¼ teaspoon
        dried thyme leaves
    5 bay leaves
    4 small tomatoes, cut into ¼-inch cubes
        (about 2 cups)
    1 medium red bell pepper, seeded and cut into
        ¼-inch cubes (about 1 cup)
    1 medium yellow bell pepper, seeded and cut
        into ¼-inch cubes (about 1 cup)
    1 medium zucchini, cut into ¼-inch cubes
        (about 2 cups)
    Freshly ground black pepper

1 Arrange the eggplant halves or slices on a plate and sprinkle the flesh sides evenly with ½ teaspoon salt. Let sit for 30 minutes. Blot the excess moisture from the eggplant with a paper towel. In a 12-inch skillet, heat 1 tablespoon of the oil over medium heat. When the oil is hot, add the eggplant, flesh side down, and fry until beginning to turn golden, 5 to 8 minutes. Flip the eggplant over and fry, adding more oil if needed, until the slices are fork-tender but not yet mushy. Transfer to a plate and set aside in a warm place.

2 Add the remaining 2 tablespoons oil to the skillet and heat over medium-low heat. Stir occasionally throughout the following process:

Add the onion, garlic, thyme, and bay leaves and cook until the onion is just translucent, about 5 minutes. Add the tomatoes and ½ teaspoon salt and cook until the tomatoes are just soft, about 8 minutes. Add both bell peppers and cook until just fork-tender, about 10 minutes. Finally, add the zucchini and cook until just fork-tender, 5 to 7 minutes. Taste for salt; add a few grinds of pepper. Discard the garlic cloves, thyme sprigs (if using) and bay leaves. Place the eggplant on a serving platter and spoon an equal amount (about ⅓ cup) of the diced vegetables over each slice. Serve at once.

Sautéed Turnips with Cinnamon
Navets à la Cannelle

Sautéing the turnips mellows their flavor, while the pinch of cinnamon adds a roasty, spicy note. This makes an ideal side dish (see photograph, page 63) for roast meats.

Serves 6

> 3 tablespoons extra-virgin olive oil
> 2 pounds medium turnips, peeled and
>   cut into 1½-inch cubes
> Salt
> ¼ to ½ teaspoon ground cinnamon
> 1 teaspoon sugar

Heat a large sauté pan over medium-high heat. Add the oil and heat until it begins to shimmer. Add the turnips and cook, stirring occasionally but not too frequently, until they begin to pick up golden spots, about 10 minutes. Stir in ½ teaspoon salt and the cinnamon, cover, lower the heat to medium-low, and cook, turning the turnips every 5 minutes, until they are tender enough to pierce with a fork but still just slightly firm in the center, 20 to 25 minutes. Stir in the sugar, mixing well, then re-cover and cook for another 5 minutes. Taste and add more salt if needed. Transfer to a serving platter and serve immediately.

Provençal-Style Braised Artichokes
Artichauts à la Provençale

This braise of artichokes, wine, bacon, and pearl onions is seasoned with fresh thyme (see photograph, page 54). Baby artichokes are mature but small artichokes (see page 196). Medium artichokes can be substituted; quarter them lengthwise.

Serves 4

> 2 pounds baby artichokes (about 10) or medium
>   artichokes (about 4), with a few inches of
>   stem intact if possible
> ¼ cup extra-virgin olive oil
> 1 cup peeled and thickly sliced carrots
> 3 ounces slab bacon, cut into lardons 2 inches
>   long and ¼ inch wide and thick (about ½ cup)
> 10 pearl onions (about 1 cup)
> 2 garlic cloves
> 1½ cups dry white wine (such as Chardonnay)
> 3 fresh or dried thyme sprigs, or ¼ teaspoon
>   dried thyme leaves
> Salt and freshly ground black pepper

Trim the artichokes of any sharp spines. In a Dutch oven, heat the oil over medium-low heat. When the oil is hot, add the artichokes to the pot, working in batches if necessary, and raise the heat to medium. Cook, stirring often, until the artichokes pick up golden patches, about 7 minutes. Transfer to a plate. With the pot still over medium heat, add the carrots, bacon, onions, and garlic to the oil and cook, stirring occasionally, for 10 minutes. Return the artichokes to the pot, add the wine and thyme, and season with salt and pepper. Cover and simmer on medium-low heat, stirring occasionally, until the liquid has reduced by about half and the bottoms of the artichokes are easily pierced with a fork, 40 to 50 minutes. Taste the sauce and add more salt if needed. Serve hot or at room temperature.

The Château de Vincennes, on the outskirts of Paris.

Fresh Fish, Superbly Sauced

Fish and Seafood

Oysters on the half shell served with nothing more than lemon, such as these from a seafood stall at Marché Bastille, are a beloved Parisian food. Page 70: Quick-Cured Sardine Fillets (page 86).

Pauline Rolland's first real adventure in the kitchen was the result of an offhand remark. She had mentioned to her husband, Yuri Zapanic, that as much as she loved the Paris neighborhood where they lived, she longed to get in touch with her roots, which are in Brittany, a region in western France. Zapanic couldn't be much help in that department, as he was born and raised in Kansas. He had a good suggestion, though: Rolland's mother, Marie, excelled at cooking classic Breton dishes. So why not ask her how to make something from their birthplace?

"But I'm not a *real* cook," Rolland had replied. A vivacious and charming woman in her thirties, she is an actress when she isn't at her university office job, and frankly, gastronomy hasn't been her top priority.

Today, however, Rolland, with her usual brio, is embarking on her mother's recipe for poached cod with beurre blanc sauce. It's a dish with cachet. The sauce, which is made of butter, wine, and cream, is considered one of the key preparations of French cuisine. It's an ambitious thing for a novice to cook, though, because it is challenging to make correctly. Beurre blanc, however, is also exceedingly delicious—silky, and shot through with tangy pickled shallots—and it is a favorite of Rolland's, so she is determined.

She has all of the ingredients laid out on the kitchen counter along with her laptop: Her mother has been walking her through the steps via video call.

"Did you pickle the shallots already?" Rolland's mother asks. Rolland tilts her laptop so that Marie can view the shallots, now minced on the cutting board.

"Well," she says, her lips making a slight *moue* of disapproval, "they could be cut more finely and uniformly, but they'll do, *chérie.*"

Rolland cooks the shallots with wine, then whisks in the cream. "Lower the heat, Pauline," her mother says with sudden urgency. "From this moment, do everything to keep the liquid from coming to a boil. Adjust the flame as often as you need to."

Under Marie's watchful eye, Rolland adds cold butter, one cube at a time, stirring constantly. "Mother, I'm afraid this isn't going to work," she frets. But, as Marie reminds her, it just takes time—and patience. And roughly ten minutes later, voilà: in the saucepan is a picture-perfect sauce, deeply golden and with a smooth texture.

Tentatively, Rolland dips a spoon in to taste. Relief. "I did it on my first attempt!" she says, grinning as her mother applauds. Then, confidence boosted, Rolland sets to poaching the cod in a broth of tarragon, parsley, bay leaves, and a splash of the same wine that went into the sauce. She cooks the fish until, according to Marie's screen-eye view, it is just done.

Rolland places the cod pieces onto a platter and ladles the sauce over it. "Oh, it looks so lovely," she says. "I can't believe I made this!"

"Well done, Pauline," Marie says, beaming. "Your grandmother would be proud."

On the other side of Paris, in a small walk-up apartment in Saint-Denis, a northern suburb usually known more for its social and economic inequality than its cooking, Bintou Coulibaly, a business-woman in her fifties, has a more practiced hand at preparing fish.

Originally from the West African nation of Mali, she has lived in Paris with her extended family for decades. But Coulibaly retains a strong connection to her birthplace and likes to call up the flavors of home by making *thiéboudienne*, a wholesome one-pot dish with Senegalese roots which is now cooked throughout West Africa. It features fish that is first slathered in a forest-green marinade of parsley and onion and panfried before being added to a comforting mélange of slow-cooked vegetables and paella-like rice. Coulibaly is far from alone in her fondness for the dish: there's hardly a person in Paris who isn't familiar with *thiéboudienne*, so frequently does it appear on the menus of West African restaurants in the city.

This morning, Coulibaly had put thick grouper steaks up to marinate. Now, humming along to music on the radio, she cooks the grouper in sizzling oil. Then she fries a pungent paste of onion and garlic, along with whole habanero chiles, and bay leaves. She adds some water and a can of tomatoes, and it becomes a braising broth with a great depth of flavor.

Just as the liquid begins to bubble, Fatima Abbas, an easygoing friend of Coulibaly's, arrives to help. The women make an excellent team in the kitchen, working in a leisurely flow in unspoken anticipation of the other's needs. Abbas cuts the carrots and cabbage into chunks while Coulibaly stems the eggplant and okra. By now the rest of the Coulibaly family is drifting into the apartment, settling onto cushions in the living room for Saturday lunch.

"It smells fantastic, Mom," calls the eldest son. Two younger kids, Coulibaly's grandchildren, chime in, saying they can't wait to eat. Coulibaly, who has commenced cooking rice in the same ambrosial broth as the vegetables, agrees. She's hungry herself, and the aroma is filling her with anticipation. She carries the steaming food into the living room. Coulibaly smiles, admiring the feast that will feed her family this afternoon.

Insider's Tips from a Paris Wine Merchant

As a wine seller in Paris, I can assure you that enjoying wine does not require big spending. On the contrary, when it comes to wine, quality doesn't have much to do with price. What really matters is the production process, from vine to bottle: where and how the wine is made, with what grapes, by whom, and when. There are plenty of good French red wines for under €15, as is the case with all the wines shown at left. **Le Petit Gascoûn**, priced around €6.50, is a good example of an inexpensive, simple red from southwest France. It is a mix of tannat and cabernet franc grapes. Grapes grown in the sunny south taste stronger, so those wines tend to be better for having with a meal than for straight-up sipping—and by the way, in Paris we traditionally serve wine with food, even if it's just a bowl of nuts. A **Winerie Parisienne Grisant Rouge** (around €13) is an easy-to-drink red, ideal for people who don't necessarily love the taste of wine, and flexible enough to go with both meat and fish. You can find other adaptable wines at a low price, such as **Bourgogne Gamay, Louis Latour**, a Pinot from Burgundy, a crowd-pleaser for only €15 that can be drunk with almost anything. Or you might pick a Syrah, like the 2015 **Crozes-Hermitage** from the Rhône valley (€15) that goes beautifully with roast meats and stews. And do yourself a favor and sample some affordable rosés. They are refreshing in warm weather and wonderful on a picnic. Rosés used to be erratic in quality, but nowadays, they're more consistently good, and there are some *really* good ones, like the **Mas Jullien** from the Loire Valley for only about €16.

You don't need to understand the intricate details of the world of viticulture to appreciate French wine. The easiest and best way to explore what wines are out there is by building a relationship with a merchant from a wine store that you trust and respect. Over time, a good wine seller will begin to understand the kinds of wines you appreciate and will be able to steer you consistently in a direction that makes you happy. Those of us who sell wine are aware of which good labels are off the beaten path, and we know when a fantastic new wine has just come on the market. Do you need a wine for a special occasion or a casual get-together? Do you need an aperitif, or perhaps something to go with dinner, and if so, what might be on the menu? What is your budget?

Simply talk to your merchant about your preferences. If you are looking for wine in the medium price range, like the ones pictured at right, you might go for a white; whites aren't necessarily costly, but you generally have to spend more on a white if you want something up to standard. Take a wine like the €35 **Petit Chablis Blanc, Auxey-Duresses**. It is a 100 percent Chardonnay from Burgundy, and it is beautiful as an aperitif or served with seafood. Or consider a moderately priced Champagne, such as **Legras** (about €30); with perfectly sized small bubbles, it pairs magnificently with a meal. And you might be interested to know that there are medium-priced red wines, such as the **Château de Rouillac** from Pessac, made of a mix of Merlot and Cabernet grapes, that are as soft in the mouth as velvet and cost only about €24.

Needless to say, if you want to spend more money, any number of truly memorable French wines will be available to you in any good wine shop. You need not break the bank completely, though. For €42, the sparkling pink **Philipponnat Champagne**, made mostly with Pinot Noir grapes, is as good as the reliably stellar **Dom Pérignon Champagne** (for a fraction of the €165 price of the latter). You could also treat yourself to a 2012 **Meursault Vieilles Vignes Sylvain Dussort,** a Burgundian white wine with delicious floral and woody notes (about €60). A good Sauternes such as a **Carmes de Rieussec** (€120), which in France is traditional to have at Christmastime with foie gras, has a sweetness that also makes it a nice dessert wine. When you're going to spend a considerably larger sum, let a merchant help you find a wine in which the excellence of a vintage and a vintner come together. For example, the Bordeaux produced by **Château Pape Clément**, a winery that is over six hundred years old, has a small but first-rate production that justifies its €190 price tag. Keep an open mind, however, as the field of wine is in constant flux. Because wines are an agricultural product, they change from year to year. This affects distribution and availability, which means a vineyard whose wines you've fallen in love with might not have enough product to sell for months and months. For example, 2011, 2015, and 2019 were terrific for Bordeaux, but there isn't much of it, due to those years' hot summers that produced few grapes. No matter what is going on in the vineyards, though, a wide range of top-notch wines is always available. That is part of the magic of French wine.
—*Christian Leblond , Paris-based wine merchant*

Quick-Cured Sardine Fillets
Sardines à la Maison

Capturing the essence of the sea in a simple salt cure, these sardines are wonderfully rewarding to make. This recipe, a classic Parisian appetizer, was adapted from one by seafood aficionado and nature-documentary presenter Jérôme Delafosse.

Serves 4

    4 fresh whole sardines
    2½ cups coarse salt (see page 195)
    ⅓ cup sugar
    4 thick slices pain au levain (French sourdough)
        or other high-quality bread
    1 Roma tomato, finely diced
    1 tablespoon minced fresh chives
    Freshly ground black pepper
    Extra-virgin olive oil

1 Fillet the sardines as directed on page 191. Rinse them under cold running water and pat them dry.

2 In a bowl, stir together the salt and sugar. On a large plate, spread enough of the salt-sugar mixture to create a ½-inch-thick layer large enough to accommodate the sardines in a single layer. Place the sardines on the salt-sugar mixture and top them with the remaining mixture, creating an even layer and covering the fish completely. Let stand at room temperature for 20 minutes. Scrape off the salt, gently rinse the sardines in cold water, and gently pat them dry with paper towels.

3 Arrange a sardine atop a slice of the bread and sprinkle with some of the tomato and chives, a grind of pepper, and a drizzle of the oil. Repeat with the remaining sardines, bread, tomato, and chives, drizzling each with oil. Serve at once.

Opposite: the exterior raw bar of Restaurant de Haute-Mer. Pages 84 to 85: West African Rice with Fish and Vegetables (page 90), both as it cooks and when complete.

An Elevated Feast

First popularized in the 1920s by the storied brasserie Le Dôme, the *plateau de fruits de mer* (seafood platter) is an array of raw and cooked shellfish on the half shell, mounded decoratively on ice or seaweed or both, and traditionally presented on an elevated serving platter. In a restaurant, this is generally ordered as a celebratory first course, but since it is not so much a dish as it is an assemblage, it can easily be adapted to make at home for a memorable group meal. Ask your trusted fishmonger for what is freshest and in season. Among the possibilities are raw oysters and clams and poached or steamed shrimp or langoustine, crab, and lobster. Clean and shuck the oysters and clams. Mound a large platter with crushed ice (you can hunt for proper multilevel serving platters online, if you like) and arrange the seafood on top in a decorative pattern. Serve with individual bowls of *sauce mignonette* (a dipping sauce made of white wine vinegar and minced shallots), plenty of quartered lemons for squeezing, and a couple of baguettes. Don't forget to put out finger bowls, each with a thin slice of lemon for your guests to clean their fingers after the feast.

Herb-Poached Fish with Beurre Blanc Sauce

Poisson au Beurre Blanc

This recipe, based on Pauline Rolland's (see photograph, page 76), is worth mastering: fish fillets poached to perfection in a wine-and-herb broth, then blanketed with a sauce in which tangy minced pickled shallots set off the rich and mellow flavors of butter and cream. It lends itself well to teamwork because it's easiest to do if one person is cooking the fish while the other is making the sauce. Be sure to prepare the pickled shallots at least a day beforehand.

Serves 4

PICKLED SHALLOTS
½ cup white wine vinegar
2 shallots, quartered
BEURRE BLANC
Salt
¼ cup dry white wine (such as Chablis)
½ cup heavy cream
Freshly ground white pepper
1 cup (2 sticks) cold unsalted butter,
   cut into 1-inch cubes
FISH
5 cups water
½ cup dry white wine (such as Chablis)
Salt
2 bay leaves
5 fresh flat-leaf parsley sprigs
2 fresh tarragon or thyme sprigs
4 black peppercorns
4 pieces skinless firm white fish fillet
   (such as cod, grouper, or hake), each
   about 6 ounces and ½ inch thick
Baguette, for serving

1 Up to a week before you make this dish, prepare the pickled shallots for the beurre blanc. In a small nonreactive bowl or glass jar, mix together the vinegar, shallots, and a pinch of salt, cover, and let sit at room temperature for at least 24 hours.

2 To make the beurre blanc, drain the pickled shallots and finely mince them. In a medium saucepan, combine the ¼ cup wine and shallots and bring to a very lively simmer over medium heat. Cook, stirring often, until the liquid has evaporated by about three-fourths, about 5 minutes. Whisking constantly, add the cream, ¼ teaspoon salt, and a pinch of pepper and bring the mixture to a boil. The moment the sauce comes to a boil, turn down the heat to the lowest possible setting. From this point forward, never allow the sauce to boil again, as it will separate if it does. Add 3 cubes of the butter while whisking constantly and adjusting the heat as necessary if the mixture threatens to boil. As soon as the first cubes of butter have melted and become incorporated, add another butter cube and keep whisking until the sauce is smooth. Repeat with the remaining butter cubes, one at a time, always whisking until the butter melts and is incorporated before adding more. When all of the butter has been added, remove the sauce from the heat. Taste for salt and adjust if needed, then cover the sauce and set aside in a warm place.

3 To poach the fish, in a large skillet, combine the water, ½ cup wine, ½ teaspoon salt, bay leaves, parsley, tarragon, and peppercorns, bring to a boil over high heat, and then turn down the heat to low. When the liquid is at a steady, gentle simmer, carefully add the fish, making sure it is fully submerged. Cook the fish, turning it once, until it is flaky and just cooked through, about 3 minutes on each side.

4 Using a slotted spatula, very gently transfer the fish to a warmed serving platter or individual plates, being careful not to bring any of the poaching liquid along with it. Pour the warm sauce over the fish and serve at once with the baguette.

Sailor-Style Mussels (page 91).

West African Rice with Fish and Vegetables

Thiéboudienne

Wholesome, savory, and satisfying, this recipe for chile-marinated, panfried fish served with a slow braise of vegetables, herbs, and rice (see photographs, pages 84 and 85) is a standard of the Parisian West African kitchen. Buy a whole fish from a fishmonger and ask to have it cut, or purchase fish steaks from a quality grocer. Traditionally this is prepared more like a paella—meaning the rice is cooked with all the other ingredients—and made with broken rice, but this version, which calls for separately cooked jasmine rice, is more foolproof.

Serves 4

FISH

1 cup loosely packed fresh flat-leaf parsley leaves

2 garlic cloves, coarsely chopped

2 shallots, coarsely chopped

2 habanero chiles (optional)

1 chicken bouillon cube

½ teaspoon ground turmeric

Salt and freshly ground black pepper

Up to 3 tablespoons water

One whole 2-pound grouper or red snapper, cleaned and cut into 2-inch-thick bone-in, skin-on steaks or 5 skin-on fillets (about 5 ounces each)

½ cup peanut or canola oil

VEGETABLES AND RICE

1 medium yellow onion, coarsely chopped

3 garlic cloves, coarsely chopped

Up to 3 tablespoons water, plus 4⅓ cups

¼ cup peanut or canola oil

2 habanero chiles (optional)

3 bay leaves

¼ cup tomato paste

1 chicken bouillon cube

1 (8-ounce) can whole tomatoes and their juice

Salt and freshly ground black pepper

8-inch segment cassava (see page 197; about 12 ounces), peeled, quartered lengthwise, cored, and cut crosswise into 4-inch chunks (optional)

2 medium carrots (about 8 ounces), peeled, halved lengthwise, and cut crosswise into 4-inch chunks

½ small green cabbage (about 1 pound), quartered, leaving the core intact

12 medium okra, stemmed

2 medium Japanese or Italian eggplants (about ½ pound), stemmed, halved lengthwise (or quartered if chunky), and cut crosswise into 4-inch chunks

1½ cups jasmine rice

A few limes, halved, for serving

1 First, make the marinade for the fish. In a blender, combine the parsley, garlic, shallots, chiles (if using), bouillon cube, turmeric, ½ teaspoon salt, and a few grinds of pepper. Blend until a coarse paste forms, adding the water as needed, 1 tablespoon at a time, to keep the blades moving. Using a spoon, slather this paste onto the two fleshy sides of each fish steak. Place on a plate, cover in plastic wrap, and refrigerate for at least 1 hour or up to overnight.

2 Next, prepare the vegetables. Wipe out the blender and to it add the onion and the garlic. Blend until you have a smooth paste, adding water as needed, 1 tablespoon at a time, to keep the blades moving. In a 5-quart Dutch oven, heat the ¼ cup oil over medium heat. When the oil is hot, fry the onion-garlic paste, stirring often, until it is no longer raw, about 4 minutes. Add the chiles (if using), bay leaves, tomato paste, and bouillon cube, mix well, and fry, mashing up the bouillon cube with the back of a spoon, for 2 minutes. Add the tomatoes and their juice, mashing the tomatoes well with the spoon, then season with salt and pepper and cook, stirring occasionally, for 5 minutes. Add 3 cups of the water and bring the liquid to a simmer, maintaining the same heat. Taste the sauce and add more salt if needed. Add the cassava (if using) and cook, covered, for 15 minutes. Add the carrots, re-cover, and cook, stirring occasionally, until fork-tender, about 30 minutes. Add the cabbage, re-cover, and cook, stirring occasionally, until fork-tender, 10 to 15 minutes. Add the okra and eggplants, re-cover, and cook until fork-tender, about 20 minutes longer. Transfer all of the vegetables to a large bowl and cover to keep warm. There should be about 1½ cups thick vegetable gravy left in the pot. Measure out 1 cup of the gravy and set the rest aside.

3 Prepare the rice. Put the rice into a fine-mesh sieve and massage it under cold running water until the water runs clear. In a medium sauce-pan, combine the rice, the remaining 1⅓ cups water, and ½ cup of the reserved gravy, stir well, and place over high heat. Bring to a boil and boil for 1 minute, then stir, cover, turn down the heat to the lowest setting, and cook for 15 minutes. Remove from the heat, quickly stir, re-cover, and let the rice steam unheated for 10 minutes. Add the remaining ½ cup gravy to the rice and then fluff the rice to mix evenly. Taste the rice and add more salt if needed.

4 Next, cook the fish. Have ready a plate lined with paper towels. In a 12-inch skillet, heat the ½ cup oil over medium-high heat. To test if the oil is ready, drop a scrap of the marinade into it; it should sizzle on contact. Working in batches if necessary, add the fish pieces and fry, turning once, until golden on both sides and just cooked through, 5 to 10 minutes on each side. Be careful when turning the fish not to break the pieces. As the fish is ready, transfer it to the paper-towel-lined plate.

5 Transfer the rice to a large, deep serving plat-ter. Arrange the vegetables on top, then quickly reheat any remaining gravy and pour it evenly over the top. Arrange the fried fish on top of the vegetables and rice and serve at once, with limes on the side for squeezing on top.

Sailor-Style Mussels
Moules Marinières

This simple dish of mussels with wine and herbs (see photograph, page 89) is based on one by Dorie Greenspan, award-winning maestra of French cooking. Serve with a crusty baguette or *frites* (french fries; see page 126 for a recipe) for soaking up the delectable juices.

Serves 4

> 4 pounds mussels
> 2 tablespoons extra-virgin olive oil
> 1 medium yellow onion, finely diced
> 6 garlic cloves, unpeeled and lightly crushed
> Salt and freshly ground black pepper
> ¾ cup dry white wine (such as Sauvignon Blanc)
> 2 fresh or dried thyme sprigs, or ¼ teaspoon dried thyme leaves
> 2 fresh or dried rosemary sprigs, or 1 teaspoon dried rosemary
> 2 fresh flat-leaf parsley sprigs
> 1 bay leaf
> 2 strips lemon zest (optional)

1 Scrub the mussels under cold running water, pulling off and discarding any beards. Place the mussels into a colander. In a large Dutch oven, heat the oil over low heat. Stir in the onion, garlic, a generous pinch of salt, and a grind of pepper and cook, stirring occasionally, until the onion begins to soften, about 3 minutes. Add the wine and raise the heat to medium. Add the thyme, rosemary, parsley, bay leaf, and lemon zest (if using) and simmer for 3 minutes longer. Add the mussels and stir. Raise the heat and bring the liquid to a boil. Cover, adjust the heat so the liquid simmers steadily, and cook for 3 minutes. Check the mussels: if most of them are still closed, cook for another 1 to 2 minutes; if most are open, turn off the heat and let them rest covered for 1 minute (or more, if need be) until the remainder open.

2 Discard any mussels that haven't opened. Serve immediately.

5

The World Capital of Dining Out

Main Dishes

Opposite: North African Lamb and Vegetable Tagine (page 123). Page 92: Braised Veal in Mushroom and Cream Sauce (page 122). Page 94: Sunday afternoon solo soccer in the Bois de Vincennes. Page 95: Salt-Roasted Pork with Preserved Lemon and Ginger (page 123).

Joséphine Chez Dumonet, a restaurant in the sixth arrondissement and in existence in one form or another since the late 1800s, is a master class in the art of bistro dining. Graciousness and warmth are evident in its every detail, from its mosaic-tiled floors and comfortable banquettes to its lighting fixtures, which cast an ambient glow. The chief idea of proper bistro service is that the customer feels at home. On this particular cold winter night, a silver-haired woman who has come to the restaurant to dine by herself is being greeted with a warm embrace by the headwaiter, a handsome fellow who helps her out of her coat.

The first order of business is to see that she is comfortably seated and has had a moment to collect herself; only then will she be solicited for her choice of water. There are a few water options, as the French diner understands that water can be its own pleasure, to be paired with a meal depending on its level of carbonation and mineral content. Wine is a whole other discussion—one that will be had after she's decided on a first course, so something complementary can be suggested.

With a contented sigh, the diner unfurls a linen napkin. Last night her brother came to visit her in her apartment, and she'd prepared a special *plat*, or main course, to celebrate the occasion. The defining quality of a French main course is that it involves not necessarily the most complicated, but certainly the most intensive, cooking. In her case, she'd made pork roasted in a salt crust. When she'd cracked the crust open at the table, revealing the roast enshrouded in steam, it had made for a theatrical presentation.

Dishes like this take some effort, but they are not haute cuisine. They are basic foods meant to be fulfilling. The diner and her brother had both relished every bite the previous night, but tonight, it's lovely to relax and let someone else do the cooking.

Across the room, a stylish woman and her two equally fashionable daughters who have flown in from Capetown to enjoy a weekend of high-end shopping in Paris are poring over the menu. Three sleek blonde heads bend over three menus as they decide on their main courses.

(continued on page 104)

The Visionary Gesture

Alain Passard is one of a handful of the great international chefs of the last two centuries—people from all walks of life in France know his name. As a restaurant critic, I've been to Passard's restaurant in Paris, Arpège, multiple times, so by now I know that his curiosity and vision have no limits. With techniques grounded in the traditional, he pushes the boundaries, always perfecting the gesture—*"la main"* (the hand), as he puts it—experimenting with the form and technique of cooking, leaning into its formal strictures at some times and pushing the envelope at others. This is why his cuisine feels timeless as well as extraordinary.

I recently dined at Arpège with Jacques Genin, one of the greatest pastry chefs in France. We were presented first with dumplings of incredibly delicate pasta holding minced-vegetable stuffing in a crystalline consommé. Then, *chaud-froid d'oeuf* (hot-cold egg), a froth served inside a carefully cut eggshell half, and lobster with a silken and rich sauce. The latter two dishes were on the menu that earned Passard his three Michelin stars in 1996.

After this came a roasted monkfish, pure and subtle, which was followed by one of Passard's signature dishes— and one of his surrealist touches: half a wild duck and half a farm-raised chicken, sewn together and roasted over hay, so both were infused with the taste of the fields in Brittany. Although the dish was visually dramatic, the flavors were essential, not fussy. Then came a small and magnificent suckling pig, cooked whole in the baker's oven and presented to us by Damien Chapron, the pastry chef at Arpège. Like a composer writing a symphony, Passard had begun our meal a few hours before with carefully orchestrated flourishes, then right in the middle of it, he abruptly changed tempo with these two straightforward, almost primal dishes: roasted meats with minimal showmanship.

(continued on page 103)

Opposite: Arpège pastry chef Damien Chapron holding Puff Pastry with Salt-Packed Anchovies. Page 100: Lunch at Arpège. Page 101: Alain Passard. Pages 102 to 103: pouring hard cider to top off the meal.

(continued from page 98)

At this point, Genin and I agreed that we couldn't possibly still be hungry. Yet somehow, when each new plate arrived, we felt *la gourmandaise*—a word that conveys a desire to eat more. So it was with delight that we greeted the course that followed, which was Chapron's work as well: *feuilleté d'anchois*, a lighter-than-air, crackly, golden piece of puff pastry layered with salt-cured anchovies and onion marmalade.

The final dish was made of that same perfectly crisp yet fluffy puff pastry, transformed into a dessert of vanilla custard, a scattering of strawberries, and syrup made from those strawberries. It was elaborate in creation but spare on the palate: fresh, sweet, buttery, flaky. In total, the approach was authentic Passard. Over the course of four and a half hours we were fed as if it were our last meal ever. And in truth, it might very well be, so why not enjoy it?
—*Jean-Bernard Magescas, author of* Mille Saveurs, *a column for the newspaper* L'Opinion

(continued from page 96)

"Hmm, I'm torn," the mother muses. "I always get steak frites, but the *tomates farcis* sound terrific." In the latter dish, tomatoes are filled with roast sirloin, shallots, parsley, rosemary, chives, oregano, and thyme—almost an entire farm on a plate. But she is not alone in habitually ordering Paris's justly celebrated version of grilled steak and French fries; it is a bistro classic for a reason. The steak is irresistible, cooked in garlicky butter.

For nearly as long as cooking itself has existed, people have been serving food to paying customers: Excavated archaeological sites illustrate that was it possible to visit take-out counters in ancient Greece, Rome, China, and Mexico. But a space dedicated to not simply the procuring of a meal, but also the ritualized process of being waited on, is a different concept altogether. And it is one which the city of Paris has singularly put on the map.

The French word *restaurant* literally means "that which restores," and the first places in France to use that term served a broth enriched with meat and egg (evidently focused more on restoring health than delighting the palate). Given the proclivity of the French for refinement, though, that particular culinary practice lasted only briefly before the first formal—and presumably more amusing—restaurant, Le Restaurant Boulanger, was established in 1765. Camille La Broue, a celebrated French food writer of the early 1900s, writes that the owner of the establishment, Monsieur Boulanger, regularly hobnobbed with the rich, "inevitably leading

them to his restaurant, with its daintily set out tables." Boulanger offered a novelty: a selection of dishes to choose from, served on demand. Sued by a local food guild for infringing on its monopoly on the sale of cooked foods, he won; this victory led to the great blossoming of restaurant culture in Paris.

In the 1780s, Antoine Beauvilliers opened La Grande Taverne de Londres, combining high-quality cooking, an extensive wine cellar, and an elegant space attended by efficient, smartly dressed waiters. After the French Revolution, when a significant number of aristocrats upped stakes and fled the capital, many of their cooks, who knew a thing or two about top-tier food service, stayed behind and opened restaurants. By the century's end, if one wanted a luxury dining experience, Paris was the place.

Now, at Chez Joséphine Dumonet, a pair of men have just come in, one fashionably tousled, the other elegantly dressed, and the headwaiter is leading them to their usual booth in the back. Their passage sets the three visitors from Capetown to whispering. This bistro is a favorite hangout of journalists, and one of the men is not a little controversial for having recently scooped an international political scandal.

"Look, but don't look like you're looking," the elder daughter advises the younger, taking a piece of baguette from a basket on the table.

The journalists, meanwhile, have more pressing concerns. Will there be, one of them wonders aloud, *blanquette de veau* (veal in mushroom sauce) on the menu tonight? He ate it this past autumn, a Sunday lunch at his aunt and uncle's house, and ever since, he's been craving a reprise of that cozy, aromatic stew of veal and vegetables. He explains that it is his relations' *specialité*. "My uncle always serves it with mashed potatoes," he concludes, adding, "I should really visit them more often."

His companion replies. "*Blanquette de veau* is very good, but for me, on a cold night like this, *confit de canard* is the ultimate." This recipe calls for thyme-and-pepper-marinated duck legs to be simmered in bubbling duck fat over a painstakingly low flame for hours. "With a glass of Bordeaux, in front of a crackling fire? There's nothing better," he adds.

A young diner at another table peeks at the journalists from behind the type of glasses that make a bold statement. "They must be discussing politics," she whispers. Her female companion nods, helping herself to a mussel from their first course, a bowl of *moules marinières* (mussels steamed in wine and herbs).

The pair have been dining out together since their college days, and by now they have their favorite things to order, depending on the place. Here, their favorite main course is the *boeuf bourguignon*, for which this particular bistro is renowned. Among main courses, this one is a pinnacle of achievement: marinated beef seasoned with onion, herbs, and bacon and cooked in a good red wine—preferably a Burgundian variety, as the dish hails from Burgundy—for hours. Like so many of the great French dishes, it is basic in theory but sublime in practice. These old friends will soon enjoy it in respectful silence.

Setting the Scene

The French art of laying a table is second to none. A "banquet setting" is the most refined method, suitable for a formal dinner with multiple courses, but you can use a more pared-down approach as a fun way to bring a French sensibility to the everyday dining table. The basic guidelines are as follows: First, be sure the environment is clean and orderly. Cover the table with a tablecloth. Adapt the silverware to what you're serving (serrated knives, for example, for steak, or soup spoons). Place forks on the left, knives on the right, and the soup spoon and dessert spoon at the top of the plate, between the plate and the glasses; a rule of thumb is that the larger items always go closest to the plate. Position the bread plate to the left of the top of the fork. Use large wineglasses for red wine and smaller wineglasses for white. Place the glasses at the top of the knife, in either a row or a triangle formation. The largest and tallest glass should be positioned on the inside. For example, from the inside to the outside, first the glass for red wine, then for white wine, and finally for water. Place a folded napkin on each dinner plate. Distribute condiments in small decorative plates, bowls, or ramekins around the table so they are easily reached by everyone. If serving food that generates scraps, such as mussel shells, olive pits, or artichoke leaves, put out bowls for capturing them. Finally, decorate the table with a vase containing the prettiest fresh flowers you can find.

Classic Roast Leg of Lamb (page 124) evokes both comfort and tradition.

"Beef is one of the greatest glories of France. Of course, there are many excellent ways to prepare it, but cooking a high-quality filet in the style of *steak frites* is simply the best method. Grill the steak in a hot pan to create a crust, place it in the oven for a few minutes, then finish it with a bath of frothy, herb-flavored butter. It reveals the true taste of meat."

—HUGO DESNOYER, BUTCHER AND RESTAURATEUR

Clockwise from upper left: Ultimate Pan-Grilled Steak and Twice-Cooked French Fries (page 126); butcher and restaurateur Hugo Desnoyer; veal tartare with caviar and without, as served at Hugo Desnoyer (for a recipe for burgers made with veal tartare, see page 127); a side of beef being carried into cold storage at Boucherie Hugo Desnoyer. Pages 110 to 111: A chilly night is no obstacle for those who like to dine outdoors.

Les Pique-niqueurs

I was raised in the countryside in central France, and when I first came to Paris as a student more than a decade ago, I was excited by the vibrancy and intensity of the city. After a time, though, I began to yearn for the quieter, more natural world I'd left behind. Then I made a wonderful discovery: Parisians love to picnic. They do it just about everywhere they can—in little pocket parks; in the sprawling, forestlike Bois de Vincennes in the city's southeast; along the cement banks of Canal Saint-Martin. So to assuage my longing to be outside, I soon began to go on as many picnics as possible. Now, my husband, Axel, and my friends often join me in the Parc des Buttes-Chaumont, which is the perfect place to picnic, as it offers both a view of the city and beautiful old trees to sit beneath. I cherish the laid-back quality of eating outdoors, but I also take it seriously. The word *pique-nique* (which originated in France) implies a meal to which everyone contributes. And indeed, on this afternoon in the park, we have all brought something good to eat or drink, making a colorful buffet on a simple cloth around which we sit. With the grass underneath and the leaves rustling overhead, I almost feel as if I were in the countryside, reconnecting with who I really am. *—Léa Pernollet, screenwriter*

This painterly scene of picnickers relaxing over an outdoor meal is a typical sight in Belleville Park.

The many summertime picnickers along the Canal Saint-Martin pay special attention to the food and drink they bring. A typical meal might include a variety of cheeses, small plates, fruits, a dessert, wine, and, of course, baguettes.

Burgundy-Style Beef Braised in Red Wine

Boeuf Bourguignon

One of the mainstays of the French culinary canon, *boeuf bourguignon* (see photograph, page viii) is Burgundian country cooking at its most delicious. Born of humble roots, it showcases a method designed to tenderize the least tender cuts of beef and infuse them with flavor by slow cooking them in wine and broth. A Burgundian red will make the very best version, but whichever wine you use, its fundamental flavor will come across mostly unchanged, so it's of paramount importance to use a wine that would impress you if you were drinking it straight from the glass. The cut of meat, too, is crucial to achieving the fall-apart tenderness that makes this meal so memorable. And for optimum results, you'll want to marinate the beef for a full day. This recipe yields a dish like that served at the restaurant Joséphine Chez Dumonet and is best accompanied by a starch that goes well with a saucy dish, such as flat noodles, boiled potatoes, or rice. To achieve the traditional thick consistency of the sauce, it's best to use a Dutch oven that is wide and shallow enough to allow moisture to evaporate easier rather than a tall, deep pot.

Serves 4

2 pounds boneless beef chuck, lightly trimmed of excess fat and cut into 2-inch cubes
One 750-ml bottle good red wine of a dark and inky type (such as Burgundy or Cabernet Sauvignon)
1 medium yellow onion, thickly sliced horizontally
1 garlic clove, minced
Bouquet garni (2 bay leaves, a few fresh or dried thyme sprigs, a few fresh or dried oregano sprigs)
Freshly ground black pepper
Salt
2 tablespoons peanut or sunflower oil, plus more as needed

4 ounces slab bacon, cut into lardons 2 inches long and ¼ inch wide and thick (about ¾ cup)
2 tablespoons all-purpose flour
1 cup French Chicken Broth (page 188)

1 In a large nonreactive bowl, combine the beef, wine, onion, garlic, bouquet garni, and 1 teaspoon pepper and stir a few times to mix well. Cover and refrigerate for at least 3 hours or preferably overnight.

2 Remove the meat from the marinade and pat it thoroughly dry with paper towels, getting it as dry as possible—this step is crucial. Season the meat with ½ teaspoon salt. Remove the onion slices from the marinade and set them and the marinade aside.

3 In a 5-quart Dutch oven, heat the oil over medium heat. Add the bacon and fry, stirring occasionally, until just golden, about 7 minutes. Using a slotted spoon, transfer the bacon to a plate. Working in batches to avoid crowding, add the beef to the fat remaining in the pot and cook over medium heat, turning as needed, until browned on all sides, about 10 minutes per batch. Add extra oil to the pot if there is insufficient fat to keep the meat frying. (If the meat releases enough liquid to stop it from browning properly, scoop out the liquid and add it to the reserved marinade.) As each batch is ready, transfer it to a plate.

4 Turn down the heat slightly, add the reserved onion slices, and fry, adding extra oil if needed and turning the slices a few times, until they are translucent and golden, about 5 minutes. Stir in the flour and mix well, scraping up the flour that sticks to the bottom of the pot. Cook until the flour begins to brown, about 2 minutes, continuously scraping the bottom of the pot. Add the reserved marinade, including the bouquet garni, and continue to stir it until all of the flour is integrated into the wine. Return the bacon and beef to the pot, pour in the broth,

Sirloin-Stuffed Tomatoes (page 127).

and mix well. Raise the heat to medium-high and bring to a boil. The moment the mixture reaches a boil, turn down the heat to the lowest setting, cover, and cook at a very gentle simmer (adjust the heat as necessary and be vigilant that it does not boil), stirring occasionally, until the sauce is becoming quite thick and the meat is extremely tender, 3 to 3½ hours.

5 Uncover the pot and continue to cook at a gentle simmer until the sauce is thick enough to coat the back of a spoon. To test if it is ready, dip a metal spoon into the sauce, then draw your finger through the sauce on the back of the spoon; the track should remain clear. The timing will depend on the depth and width of the pot, but should take roughly 15 minutes before serving.

Duck Confit with Fingerling Potatoes

Confit de Canard

Native to Gascony in the south of France, the cooking method of this dish—a form of charcuterie—was originally used during duck hunting season as a way to preserve the bounty of game so it would last through the winter. Traditionally slow cooked in duck fat over very low heat, the duck legs become somewhat caramelized and pull-apart tender, with a salty, rustic flavor. This version calls for cooking in duck or pork fat and is spectacular served with potatoes and a garnish of chives. To get it right, it's essential to marinate the duck for 48 hours before cooking. Confit reheats well in an oven or a skillet, though leftovers are delicious eaten at room temperature—or minced and used in a salad with asparagus (see page 34).

Serves 4

Salt and coarsely ground black pepper
2 tablespoons fresh thyme leaves, or
   1 tablespoon dried thyme leaves
4 whole duck legs, trimmed of excess fat
8 cups rendered duck fat or pork lard
   (about 4 pounds), plus more as needed
3 fresh or dried thyme sprigs (optional)
3 bay leaves
1 medium yellow onion, quartered
6 garlic cloves, bruised
1½ pounds small fingerling or Yukon gold
   potatoes (about 5 cups), unpeeled
1 tablespoon minced fresh chives

1 In a small bowl, stir together 3 tablespoons salt, 1 tablespoon pepper, and the thyme leaves. Put the duck legs into a medium glass or ceramic bowl, sprinkle the salt mixture over the top, and massage the mixture into their surface. Cover and refrigerate for 24 hours.

2 Pour off any accumulated liquid from the duck. Massage the same salt mixture, which will have clumped and crystallized, back into the duck. Re-cover the bowl, return it to the refrigerator, and marinate for another 24 hours.

3 Remove the duck legs from the bowl and discard the accumulated liquid. Blot the excess salt and moisture from the duck with a cloth or paper towel. In a 5-quart Dutch oven, heat 3 tablespoons of the duck fat over medium heat. Working in batches if needed to avoid crowding, add the duck legs and cook, turning once, until browned on both sides, 8 to 10 minutes on each side. Transfer to a plate.

4 Turn down the heat to low, add the remaining duck fat to the pot, and heat, stirring, until the fat has fully melted. Add the duck legs, thyme sprigs (if using), bay leaves, onion, and garlic. If the duck legs are not completely submerged in the fat, add more fat as needed. Taking care to monitor the heat, cook uncovered over the lowest heat setting for 1½ hours, turning the meat every 30 minutes or so. Make sure the pot is always at a very slow simmer, with the fat at a very lazy bubble. Add the potatoes and continue to cook until the meat is beginning to pull away from the bone and feels tender when pierced with a knife and the potatoes are fork-tender, 1 to 1¼ hours longer.

5 Using a slotted spoon, remove the duck legs and potatoes from the fat to a platter or four dinner plates. Garnish with the chives and serve warm. (If you like your potatoes more browned, once they are tender, you can brown them separately in a skillet in a little leftover fat or in olive or peanut oil.) Leftover duck confit can be stored immersed in its leftover cooking fat in a nonreactive airtight container in the refrigerator for up to a few weeks. To store the duck fat or pork lard for other usages, such as making another batch of confit or using it to replace butter as a sautéing fat, pass the warmed liquid fat through a fine-mesh sieve, then store in a nonreactive airtight container in the refrigerator for up to a month or in the freezer for up to 6 months.

Roast Veal with Shallot Gravy
Veau de Grand-mère aux Échalotes

Tender, slightly sweet with caramelized shallots, and accompanied by a *jus* that comes directly from the pot, this is a traditional and rewarding method of roasting veal (see photograph, page xxii). This recipe comes from Bénédict Beaugé's grandmother, who was known for her Sunday afternoon roasts with crackly, browned exteriors and savory drippings. You can make this dish with a different bone-in cut of meat, such as a pork leg, though you will need to adjust the cooking time. Whatever you choose will be impressive served with a lettuce-and-herb salad and a bit of Dijon mustard on the side.

Serves 6

> 1 tablespoon peanut or sunflower oil
> 3 tablespoons unsalted butter
> 1 bone-in veal center leg roast or hind saddle, about 4 pounds
> Salt and freshly ground black pepper
> 2 cups coarsely chopped shallots
> 1 tablespoon coarsely chopped garlic cloves
> 2 tablespoons all-purpose flour

1 Preheat the oven to 350°F. In a 5-quart oven-safe Dutch oven, heat the oil with the butter over medium-high heat. Generously season the meat with salt and pepper. When the fat is hot, add the meat and, taking care to keep the fat from burning by raising or lowering the fire, brown it on all sides, about 10 minutes total. Cover the meat with the shallots and garlic and then sprinkle the flour evenly over the top. Cover the pot, place it inside the oven, and cook for 20 minutes.

2 Remove the lid and turn the meat over. Stir any *jus* in the pot well to integrate the flour and shallots into the gravy forming in the pot. Cover and continue to cook for 30 to 40 minutes longer, checking occasionally to be sure the sauce is not drying out. If it begins to dry out, add a small amount of water, 1 tablespoon at a time, and stir it in. The roast is done if, when you cut into it, the juices run clear, or if a thermometer inserted into the thickest part away from bone registers 155°F.

3 Transfer the veal to a cutting board, tent with aluminum foil, and let rest for 15 minutes. Cut the meat into 2- to 3-inch chunks, discarding the bone. Decant the pan juices into a gravy boat and serve it at once alongside the roast.

Opposite: Chicken Braised in Red Wine with Mushrooms (page 132). Above: French Shepherd's Pie (page 133).

Braised Veal in Mushroom and Cream Sauce

Blanquette de Veau

A quintessential French dish, this stew of meltingly tender veal and vegetables (see photograph, page 92) is bathed in a silky white sauce. It is the star of a traditional Sunday afternoon lunch and also welcome on a chilly evening when comfort is craved. Serve alongside noodles, mashed or boiled potatoes, or rice.

Serves 4

- 2 pounds boneless veal shoulder or veal rump roast, cut into 3-inch pieces
- Bouquet garni (2 bay leaves, 2 fresh or dried thyme sprigs, 2 fresh or dried oregano sprigs)
- 1 large yellow onion, quartered
- 1 leek, white part only, halved lengthwise
- 8 cups water
- Salt
- 2 medium carrots, peeled, quartered lengthwise, and cut into 2-inch-thick chunks
- 5 tablespoons unsalted butter
- 5 ounces medium cremini or button mushrooms, quartered (about 2 cups)
- 3 tablespoons all-purpose flour
- Freshly ground white or black pepper
- 1 egg yolk
- ⅓ cup heavy cream
- 1 tablespoon minced fresh flat-leaf parsley

1 In a 4-quart Dutch oven, combine the veal, bouquet garni, onion, leek, water, and 1 teaspoon salt and bring to a boil over high heat. Turn down the heat to medium-low, skim off any foam that forms on the surface, then cover partially and cook at a steady simmer until the meat is nearly tender, about 1 hour.

2 Add the carrots to the pot, re-cover partially, and cook until the meat is fully tender and the carrots are just fork-tender, 10 to 15 minutes. Using a slotted spoon, transfer the meat and carrots to a bowl, cover, and set aside in a warm place. Reduce the liquid in the pot by about half by raising the heat to medium-high and cooking uncovered, about 1 hour. Strain the liquid through a fine-mesh sieve, discarding the bouquet garni, onion, and leek, and set aside. You should have about 2 cups of broth remaining.

3 Meanwhile, in a medium skillet, melt 1 tablespoon of the butter over medium-high heat. Add the mushrooms and cook, stirring often, until they are fork-tender, 5 to 7 minutes. Set them aside with the meat and carrots.

4 In a medium saucepan, melt the remaining 4 tablespoons butter over medium-low heat. Add the flour and whisk until the mixture begins to simmer. Remove from the heat and, whisking continuously and briskly, slowly pour in the reserved 2 cups veal broth until completely incorporated. Return the pan to medium-low heat and bring the sauce to a simmer, whisking frequently. Continue to simmer, whisking frequently, until the sauce is thickened, 5 to 10 minutes. Season with salt and pepper and remove from the heat.

5 In a medium bowl, whisk together the egg yolk and cream until blended. Very slowly drizzle in about 1 cup of the sauce from the pan, whisking constantly (the slowness prevents the egg from curdling). Add this mixture to the remaining sauce in the pan and stir gently. Turn on the heat to low and stir the sauce constantly, being careful not to bring it to a simmer, until it is thick enough to coat the back of a spoon, about 5 minutes. To test if it is ready, dip a metal spoon into the sauce, then draw your finger through the sauce on the back of the spoon; the track should remain clear.

6 When the sauce is the correct consistency, transfer it to a larger pot placed over the lowest possible heat. Add the meat, carrots, and mushrooms and stir gently to combine; warm the ingredients for a few minutes. Transfer to a serving platter. Garnish with the parsley and serve immediately.

Salt-Roasted Pork with Preserved Lemon and Ginger

Carré de Porc en Croûte de Sel

Although the amount of salt used in this recipe may look alarming, it is primarily used to seal the meat in a moist cooking environment, resulting in a juicy roast that only absorbs enough salt to season it (see photograph, page 95). *Gros sel*, or coarse gray sea salt, is ideal, though kosher salt can be used.

Serves 6

> 1 cup loosely packed flat-leaf parsley leaves
> 3 or 4 slices North African Preserved Lemon (page 195) or store-bought preserved lemon, rinsed
> 4 garlic cloves
> 2-inch piece fresh ginger, peeled and sliced against the grain
> ¼ cup extra-virgin olive oil
> 1 bone-in pork loin, about 3½ pounds (which should be 6 bones)
> 2 pounds medium-coarse salt (see page 195)
> ¼ to ½ cup water

1 Coarsely chop the parsley, preserved lemon, and garlic. Transfer the mixture along with the sliced ginger to a food processor, then pulse the ingredients while streaming in the oil until a thick paste forms.

2 Blot the surface of the pork dry with paper towels. Coat the pork with the garlic-herb paste, rubbing and pressing it into the meat to help it adhere. Wrap the meat tightly in plastic wrap, working out any air bubbles that form between the meat and the wrapping. Refrigerate for 24 hours.

3 About 2½ hours before serving time, preheat the oven to 300°F. Pour the salt into a large, low roasting pan, sprinkle it with the water (starting with ¼ cup), and mix together until the mixture adheres to itself—it should have the consistency of wet sand; add a little more water as needed. Push most of the salt to one side of the pan, leaving a ½-inch-thick layer on the bottom of the pan. Unwrap the pork, leaving the garlic-herb paste undisturbed, and place the pork on its side on the bed of salt. Use the remaining salt to completely cover the meat in a ½-inch-thick layer, compressing it well to completely seal the surface.

4 Roast the pork until an instant-read thermometer inserted into the thickest part away from bone registers 140°F, 1½ to 2 hours. If you cut into the meat, the juice may run faintly pink, which is fine; as long as the thermometer reading is achieved, the meat will be correctly cooked.

5 Let the meat rest for about 10 minutes before serving. To serve, remove the salt crust in chunks if possible, then, using a pastry brush, brush away any remaining salt from the surface of the pork. Transfer the meat to a cutting board and slice the roast into individual bone-in chops. Serve immediately.

North African Lamb and Vegetable Tagine

Tagine d'Agneau

Tagine refers to both the spiced Moroccan stew (see photograph, page 97) and the wide, shallow clay cooking pot with a conical lid in which the dish is traditionally prepared. Luckily, a Dutch oven works nearly as well to produce this recipe, which is based on one from Restaurant Jour et Nuit in the Goutte d'Or neighborhood of Paris. With the appealing aroma of preserved lemons and the zing of green olives, it showcases the flavors of North Africa and makes a stellar main course. It is traditionally served with baguette to mop up the rich, spiced sauce.

Serves 4

> 2 tablespoons extra-virgin olive oil
> 1 medium yellow onion, thickly sliced into rings
> 2 garlic cloves, coarsely chopped
> 1½ pounds boneless lamb shoulder, trimmed of excess fat and cut into 3-inch chunks
> 2 tablespoons ground turmeric
> 1 tablespoon ground ginger

Large pinch of saffron threads

1½ teaspoons ground cumin

Salt

½ cup loosely packed coarsely chopped fresh
flat-leaf parsley

4 cups water

4 medium russet or other starchy potatoes
(about 1½ pounds), peeled and each cut
lengthwise into sixths

1 medium carrot, peeled and cut into 1½-inch
lengths (about 1 cup)

3 thick slices North African Preserved Lemon
(page 195) or store-bought preserved lemon,
rinsed, seeded, and cut into ¼-inch pieces

1 cup haricots verts or young, thin green beans,
trimmed and cut into 2-inch lengths

½ cup fresh or frozen peas

1 cup drained small green olives (such as
Picholine), with or without pits

Freshly ground black pepper

1 In a Dutch oven, heat the oil over medium heat.
Add the onion and cook, turning as needed, until
translucent, about 5 minutes. Add the garlic and
cook, stirring occasionally, until it is just beginning to soften, about 2 minutes. Add the lamb and
cook, turning as needed, until lightly browned
on all sides, about 3 minutes. Add the turmeric,
ginger, saffron, cumin, ½ teaspoon salt, and the
parsley, stir to mix well, and cook, stirring occasionally, for 2 minutes. Add 2 cups of the water
and mix well. Turn down the heat to the lowest
setting and bring the stew to a gentle, steady simmer. Cover and cook, stirring occasionally and
taking care that the mixture does not boil, until
the meat is very tender, about 1¼ hours or more.

2 Add the potatoes, carrot, preserved lemon,
and the remaining 2 cups water and stir to mix.
Re-cover and cook, stirring occasionally, until
the potatoes are just fork-tender, about 30 minutes. Add the haricots verts and peas and cook,
stirring occasionally, until all of the vegetables
are very tender but not mushy, about 45 minutes.

3 Add the olives and continue to cook the stew,
uncovered, just enough to warm the olives
through, about 2 minutes longer. Taste the
sauce for salt and add more if needed. Season
with pepper, stir to mix well, and serve.

Classic Roast Leg of Lamb

Gigot d'Agneau

It's a typical Parisian Easter scene: the sound of
church bells, the good Sunday table linens, and
the delicious aroma of the traditional roast leg
of lamb (see photograph, page 106) infused with
garlic and rosemary, served with simple stewed
white beans and *gratin dauphinois* (see page 64).
If you like, you can add three or four anchovy
fillets that have been coarsely chopped along
with the garlic batons and rosemary; these will
dissolve as they cook, adding umami to the
flavor of the meat and its pan juices.

Serves 8

1 bone-in leg of lamb, 7 to 8 pounds, trimmed
of excess fat

1½ heads garlic, cloves separated, half unpeeled
and half peeled and cut lengthwise into
matchstick-thick pieces

1 tablespoon fresh or dried rosemary needles

Salt and freshly ground black pepper

3 tablespoons herbes de Provence

3 tablespoons extra-virgin olive oil

1 Preheat the oven to 450°F. With the tip of a
sharp knife, poke slits about 1 inch apart and
1 inch deep all over the meat. Stuff each slit with
a piece of garlic and a rosemary needle or two.
In a small bowl, stir together 1½ teaspoons each
salt and pepper and the 3 tablespoons herbes
de Provence. Rub the oil over the entire surface
of the meat. Sprinkle the herb mixture evenly
over the oiled surface and then massage it into
the surface of the meat.

2 Put the unpeeled garlic into a roasting pan
and place the lamb on top of the garlic. Roast the
lamb, turning it three or four times and basting
with pan juices, about 1½ hours or a bit longer,

Quiche Lorraine (page 135)

until an instant-read thermometer inserted into the thickest part away from bone registers 125°F for medium rare or 135°F for medium.

3 Transfer the lamb to a cutting board, tent with aluminum foil, and let rest for 15 minutes. Carve the leg and serve at once along with the roast garlic cloves and with the pan juices in a gravy boat.

Ultimate Pan-Grilled Steak and Twice-Cooked French Fries

Steak Frites à la Hugo Desnoyer

This method yields a perfect steak, skillet-braised in garlicky, herb-inflected butter and served with French fries that are fluffy on the inside and golden crisp on the outside (see photograph, page 109). The recipe is based on one from celebrated butcher Hugo Desnoyer, who advises that you hew faithfully to these guidelines: use a European-style butter, which lends authentic flavor; only turn the meat when instructed, and use tongs rather than a fork to avoid losing any of the delicious juice. Served with red wine and Dijon mustard, it makes an uncomplicated yet decidedly romantic dinner for two.

Serves 2

> 2 filets mignons, about 8 to 10 ounces each and
>   1½- to 2-inches thick
> 4 medium russet potatoes, cut into sticks
>   3½ inches long by ¼ inch wide and thick
>   (about 4 cups)
> Peanut or canola oil, for deep-frying,
>   plus 1 tablespoon
> Salt and freshly ground black pepper,
>   preferably fleur de sel
> 2 tablespoons unsalted butter, preferably
>   European-style
> 2 fresh rosemary sprigs or 1 teaspoon
>   dried rosemary needles, optional
> 2 fresh thyme sprigs or ½ teaspoon
>   dried thyme, optional
> 2 garlic cloves, gently bruised
> Dijon mustard, for serving

1 About 1½ hours before serving, let the steaks come to room temperature. In a large bowl, cover the potatoes with water and let them rest for 30 minutes.

2 Heat oven to 450°F. If you don't have an oven-proof skillet, place a roasting pan or baking sheet on the center rack. Drain the potatoes and pat them dry thoroughly. Add the oil to a depth of 2 inches into a medium saucepan and heat over medium-high heat to 330°F on a deep fry thermometer. When the oil is ready, add about half of the potatoes and deep-fry them for 2 minutes; they will be pale golden. Using a slotted spoon, transfer the potatoes to a plate. Repeat with the remaining potatoes. Let the potato batches cool for 10 to 15 minutes.

3 Reheat the oil over medium-high heat to 365°F. When it is ready, add about half of the cooked potatoes and deep-fry them again, moving them often, until golden brown, 7 to 10 minutes. Using a slotted spoon, transfer them to a towel-lined plate to drain, then season them with salt. Repeat with the remaining potatoes and keep the French fries in a warm oven.

4 Heat a heavy 12-inch skillet (cast iron works best) over high heat until it just begins to smoke, about 5 minutes. Meanwhile coat each steak generously on both sides with about 1 teaspoon salt and do the same with a generous quantity of coarse, freshly ground pepper. Add 1 tablespoon of oil to the skillet and, using a spatula, disperse the oil around the bottom of the pan.

5 Using tongs, place the steaks in the pan and cook undisturbed for at least 2½ minutes. Gently try to lift them. If they cling to the pan at all, let them cook about 30 seconds to 1 minute more. Once they have released fully from the pan, the cooked side should be a deep golden, almost brown color. Flip them over and cook undisturbed for 2 minutes.

6 Transfer the pan to a center rack in the oven (or, if not using cast iron, place the steaks in the roasting pan or baking sheet). Cook for 4 minutes for a rare steak, 6 minutes for a medium; when juices start beading on the surface, it's just medium-rare. The cooking process will continue as the steaks rest, so you want it to be slightly less done than is to your taste.

7 Return the hot pan to the stove, but don't ignite the heat. Add the butter, the rosemary and thyme (if using), and the garlic cloves. Tip the pan toward yourself, then use a soup spoon to continuously ladle the hot, foamy butter over the steaks for about 90 seconds, lifting them occasionally so the butter also coats the bottom of the meat.

8 Remove the steaks to a plate along with their pan juices, cover them in foil, and rest them for 10 minutes. Serve at once with the French fries and the mustard.

Veal Burgers with Shallots
Tartare Aller-Retour a l'Echalote

The same ingredients that go into veal tartare—a specialty of Hugo Desnoyer's made with hand-cut raw tenderloin seasoned with shallots and chives—adapt beautifully into this cooked version, which has a delicate texture and a refined flavor. In France, a cooked patty made with tartare is called a *tartare aller-retour,* and it is best served with a side of Dijon mustard and a crusty baguette. Needless to say, you'll want to use a high-quality meat (for more on veal, see page 188).

Serves 2

    9 ounces ground veal
    2 tablespoons finely minced shallot
    1 tablespoon extra virgin olive-oil
    1 tablespoon finely minced fresh chives
    Salt
    1 tablespoon peanut or canola oil
    Baguette, for serving
    Dijon mustard, for serving

1 In a medium bowl combine the ground veal, shallot, olive oil, chives, and salt to taste (¼ to ½ teaspoon should be right) and mix well until well blended. Divide the mixture into four equal portions and shape each portion into a small patty; set aside.

2 Heat a heavy skillet (preferably cast iron) over high heat until it just begins to smoke, about 5 minutes. When the skillet is hot, add the peanut oil and, using a spatula, make sure the entire surface is covered by it. Add the patties and cook, undisturbed, until they are seared on the outside. Cook 1 minute per side, for rare, or 2 minutes per side, for medium rare. Serve at once with the Dijon mustard and baguette on the side.

Sirloin-Stuffed Tomatoes
Tomates Farcis

In summertime, when gardens are bountiful and good tomatoes call out to be used inventively, this take on a traditional Parisian home meal is just the thing: tomatoes filled with a force-meat of ground roast sirloin, shallot, garlic, and a panoply of fragrant herbs (see photograph, page 117). Savory and satisfying, it can be served as a main course with a salad, as an accompaniment to pasta, or on its own. The recipe calls for beefsteak tomatoes, but you can use any type, as long as they're big enough to hold the stuffing. You can also replace the roasted sirloin in step 4 with an equal amount of raw ground beef, veal, or pork—or a combination of the three..

Serves 5

    1 pound boneless beef sirloin
    Salt and freshly ground black pepper
    1 tablespoon peanut or canola oil
    5 medium beefsteak or other large tomatoes
    1 cup cut-up stale baguette with crust,
        in ½-inch pieces
    1 cup whole milk
    1 tablespoon finely chopped fresh
        flat-leaf parsley

Solemn and Sweet

This Passover, more than twenty of us have shown up for my friend Mivsam's seder, along with just as many kids, and everyone has brought a dish to share. Mivsam is my closest friend in Paris—she's from Israel; I'm from Poland—and I love coming to her home in Montreuil, just outside the city's eastern limits, to visit. Her house and the things that decorate its garden are colorful like a circus, and I always kind of expect an acrobat to come sliding down a rope or a lion tamer to appear from behind the fig tree. My five-year-old son, Joseph, and I join the others to sit outside at a long table lit by candles. Our Argentinian friends play their guitars, and Mivsam, who studied at Juilliard and works as a musician, joins in, playing haunting Israeli folk music on her violin. Owen and Avitale read the Haggadah—the text of Passover—aloud. Only some of us are Jewish, but all of us want to hear the story of the Israelites' liberation from Egypt. Meanwhile, the table, as if by magic, is becoming covered with plates of food, and the Parisian garden suddenly smells like a Polish shtetl during Passover a century ago. Horseradish bites the nose. The sour beet soup with cinnamon intrigues and stimulates the appetite. The chicken broth served with matzo balls comforts with its homey aroma. Sweet flourless cheesecake with almond crust and lemon zest brings delight. We pray, laugh, sing, and eat. We have cooked for one another what our grandmothers and great-grandmothers likely used to cook. The dishes I made—the cheesecake and the horseradish—are like a bridge for the other people of Polish ancestry at the table, one that leads back to the villages their families had to escape. It is the same for me. Although we live in Paris far from our families, we all feel at home. —*Ania Pamula, a Paris-based journalist*

Six-year-old Onyx Hebinger-Noiman at an outdoor seder in Montreuil munches on a round of matzoh. Pages 130 to 131: Mivsam Noiman plays the violin, while Onyx, her daughter, looks on. Far left, Onyx's twin sister, Palma Hebinger-Noiman, sits on her father's lap.

1 tablespoon finely chopped fresh tarragon
   (optional)
1½ teaspoons finely chopped fresh rosemary
   needles or ½ teaspoon finely chopped
   dried rosemary needles
1½ teaspoons fresh thyme leaves or 1 teaspoon
   dried thyme leaves
1 tablespoon finely chopped fresh oregano or
   1 teaspoon dried oregano
1 tablespoon finely chopped fresh chives
3 tablespoons finely minced shallot
2 garlic cloves, finely minced
2 tablespoons extra-virgin olive oil

1 The day before serving, preheat the oven to 375°F. Season the sirloin on all sides with salt and pepper. In a large heavy skillet, heat the peanut oil over medium-high heat. When the oil is hot, add the sirloin and sear, turning as needed, until browned on all sides, 7 to 12 minutes. Transfer the meat to a roasting pan just large enough to accommodate it and roast until an instant-read thermometer inserted into the thickest part registers 135°F, 25 to 30 minutes. The meat should be just medium when cut into with a knife. Transfer the meat to a plate, let cool slightly, then cover with plastic wrap and refrigerate overnight. (If you have not planned ahead, refrigerate the meat until cool, at least 1 hour.)

2 The next day, cut off the top 1 inch or so from each tomato, reserving the tops. One at a time, hold each tomato upside down over a bowl and gently squeeze it, coaxing out the seeds and pulp with your fingertips; discard the seeds and pulp. Sprinkle the inside of each tomato with a pinch of salt. Set them aside at room temperature, cut side up, for 30 minutes. At that point, excess liquid will have gathered inside each, so turn them over again and shake out the accumulated liquid and any remaining seeds.

3 Cut the roasted sirloin into 2-inch cubes, including any fat. In a medium bowl, combine the baguette and milk and let soak until the bread is soft and saturated, 30 seconds or so. Gently squeeze out as much milk as you can.

4 In a food processor, combine the sirloin, soaked baguette, parsley, tarragon (if using), rosemary, thyme, oregano, chives, shallot, garlic, ½ teaspoon salt, and a few grinds of pepper and process until a pâté-like texture forms. Taste for salt and pepper and add more if needed.

5 Preheat the oven to 375°F. Select a baking dish large enough to hold the tomatoes in a single layer and oil it with 1 tablespoon of the olive oil. Stuff each tomato with about ½ cup of the meat mixture, creating a rounded dome about ¼ inch high. Arrange the tomatoes in the prepared dish and top each tomato with its reserved top. Drizzle the remaining 1 tablespoon olive oil evenly over the tomatoes.

6 Bake the tomatoes until the tops are browned, about 50 minutes. Serve immediately, or serve later as a room-temperature main course.

Chicken Braised in Red Wine with Mushrooms
Coq au Vin

It need hardly be said that this hearty braise of chicken, bacon, and mushrooms cooked in wine (see photograph, page 120) is an essential French dish: virtually every home cook in France makes some version of it. It is most typically prepared with red Burgundy wine, but experimentation is encouraged, with the caveat that the taste of this dish hinges on the quality of the wine, so choose wisely. This particular recipe is inspired by one served at Chez Valentin, a homey bistro in Paris's Belleville neighborhood. Serve it the traditional way, with boiled potatoes to slather with the heavenly sauce.

Serves 4
   1 whole small chicken, 4 to 5 pounds, cut
      into pieces and each breast halved, or
      4 pounds whole legs (thigh and drumstick),
      separated at the joint
   Salt and freshly ground black pepper
   3 tablespoons peanut or canola oil

4 ounces slab bacon, cut into lardons 2 inches long and ¼ inch wide and thick (about ¾ cup)

1 cup finely chopped yellow onion

1 cup peeled and sliced carrot, in ¼-inch-thick half-moons

3 tablespoons all-purpose flour

3 cups dry red wine (such as a strong Bordeaux)

1 cup French Chicken Broth (page 188)

2 tablespoons tomato paste

Bouquet garni (2 bay leaves, a few fresh or dried thyme sprigs, a few fresh or dried oregano sprigs)

2 to 3 tablespoons unsalted butter, or as needed

1 pound medium cremini or button mushrooms, quartered

1½ pounds small fingerling or Yukon gold potatoes, boiled, peeled, buttered, and kept warm

1 Season the chicken pieces with salt and pepper, and set aside. In a 5-quart Dutch oven, heat the oil over medium heat. Add the bacon and fry, stirring occasionally, until just golden and most of the fat has rendered, about 7 minutes. Using a slotted spoon, transfer the bacon to a plate, leaving the fat in the pot.

2 Increase the heat to medium high. Working in batches, add as many chicken pieces as will comfortably fit in the pan without crowding and fry, turning as needed, until they are a deep golden color on all sides, about 7 minutes. Using tongs, transfer the chicken to a plate. Repeat with the remaining chicken pieces.

3 With the pot still over medium-high heat, add the onion and carrot and cook, stirring occasionally, until the vegetables are just tender, about 10 minutes. Stir in the flour, mixing well, and turn down the heat to low. Cook, stirring constantly, until the flour begins to turn light brown, about 5 minutes. Add the wine, broth, tomato paste, and bouquet garni and mix well, then raise the heat to high and bring the mixture to a boil, stirring occasionally. Quickly return the bacon and the chicken and its accumulated juices to the pot and return the mixture to a boil. The moment the mixture reaches a boil, turn down the heat to the lowest setting, cover, and cook, adjusting the heat as needed to keep the liquid at a slow, steady simmer, until the chicken is tender and cooked through, 25 to 35 minutes.

4 Using tongs, transfer the chicken to a bowl, cover, and set aside in a warm place. Remove and discard the bouquet garni. Raise the heat to medium and bring the sauce to a steady bubble, uncovered. Reduce the sauce until it is thick enough to coat the back of a spoon, about 10 minutes. To test if it is ready, dip a metal spoon into the sauce, then draw your finger through the sauce on the back of the spoon; the track should remain clear. Taste for salt and add more if needed. Remove from the heat and keep warm.

5 In a separate pot large enough to hold the chicken and its sauce, melt the butter over medium heat. Add the mushrooms and cook, stirring occasionally, until just fork-tender, about 8 minutes. Add the cooked chicken and the sauce and heat until the chicken is warmed through and the sauce is hot. Serve immediately with the warm buttered potatoes on the side.

French Shepherd's Pie
Hachis Parmentier

This popular French casserole of mashed potatoes over seasoned ground beef (see photograph, page 121) is based on a recipe by home cook Diane Reungsorn; her secret ingredient is a splash of Chinese oyster sauce, which is optional but lends character. The dish gets its French name from Antoine-Augustin Parmentier, who began a campaign in the early 1800s to promote potato consumption among his compatriots. The French showed their newfound love of the vegetable by creating dishes like this one. It pairs beautifully with a crisp green salad.

Serves 4 to 6

2 large Yukon gold or medium russet potatoes (about 1 pound), unpeeled

4 tablespoons unsalted butter, at room temperature

Salt

¾ cup heavy cream

2 tablespoons peanut or canola oil

1 medium yellow onion, finely chopped

3 garlic cloves, finely chopped

1½ tablespoons all-purpose flour

1 pound ground beef

Freshly ground black pepper

½ tablespoon Chinese oyster sauce (optional)

Pinch of freshly grated nutmeg

1¼ cups very dry white wine (such as Sancerre)

1 Bring a large saucepan of salted water to a boil. Add the potatoes and cook until very tender, about 50 minutes. Drain, reserving ¼ cup of the cooking liquid. Let the potatoes cool until they can be handled, then peel them and transfer to a medium bowl.

2 Using a handheld mixer or a masher, mash the potatoes, gradually adding the butter, 1 tablespoon at a time, as you work. When the butter is fully incorporated, add ½ teaspoon salt and continue to mash the potatoes, drizzling in the cream and 2 tablespoons of the cooking water until they are fully incorporated and you have a silky-smooth puree. Taste for salt and add more if needed. Cover and set aside in a warm place.

3 Preheat the oven to 425°F. In a 12-inch skillet, heat the oil over medium heat. Add the onion and cook, stirring occasionally, until tender and golden, about 7 minutes. Add the garlic and cook, stirring occasionally, until tender, 2 to 3 minutes. Stir in the flour and cook, stirring constantly, until it is just beginning to turn golden, about 3 minutes. Add the beef and a few grinds of pepper and cook, breaking up the meat with a spoon, until browned and no pink remains, about 10 minutes. Add the oyster sauce (if using), nutmeg, and wine and continue to cook, stirring occasionally, until the liquid has reduced by half, about 10 minutes. Taste and add more salt and pepper if needed.

Roast Chicken and Potatoes (page 136).

4 Transfer the contents of the skillet to a 13 by 9-inch baking dish. Spread the mashed potatoes evenly on top of the beef mixture; ideally the layers are of equal depth. Bake until the surface of the potatoes is lightly and evenly browned, about 40 minutes. Serve hot.

Quiche Lorraine

An open tart filled with a custard-like mixture of eggs, cream, and bacon, quiche Lorraine (see photograph, page 125) originated centuries ago in what is now northeastern France as a simple winter dish that could be made from ingredients that would have been readily available in nearly any household. There are many recipes for quiche Lorraine that include ingredients such as cheese, but when you taste the spare original filling, you'll understand why this is the version to make.

Serves 4

Half batch Flaky Tart Pastry (page 194)

All-purpose flour, for the work surface

4 ounces slab bacon, cut into ¼-inch cubes (about ¾ cup)

5 eggs, lightly beaten

2⅓ cups heavy cream

Salt and freshly ground white or black pepper

¼ teaspoon freshly grated nutmeg

1 Have ready the pastry dough. Fifteen minutes before baking, remove the dough disk from the refrigerator, unwrap, and dust lightly with flour. Preheat the oven to 375°F. Have ready an 11-inch tart pan or a 9½-inch pie plate. On a lightly floured work surface, roll out the dough disk, working from the center outward and rotating it clockwise a quarter turn after every few passes, until you have a round about 13½ inches in diameter and ¼ inch thick. If the dough is breaking or cracking, it's too cold; wait a few minutes for it to reach room temperature. If it begins to stick (a sign it is too warm), dust it with a tiny bit of flour. To lift the pastry easily into the pan, place the pan next to it. Set the rolling pin in the center of the round, fold half the dough

over it, and then lift the pin to place the dough into the pan. Gently press the dough onto the bottom and up the sides of the pan. If necessary, trim the overhang to make it even. Then fold the overhang inward and press along the edge with the tines of a fork, flute the edge with your fingers, or press it flat against the sides. Prick the bottom with a fork about twenty times. Line the crust with an 11-inch piece of parchment paper or waxed paper and fill the crust with pie weights or about 2 cups dried uncooked beans (such as black beans).

2 Bake the crust until dry to the touch and lightly golden, about 15 minutes. Transfer to a cooling rack, remove the weights and parchment, and let cool.

3 While the crust bakes and cools, in a heavy skillet over medium heat, fry the bacon, stirring occasionally, until almost all the fat has rendered but the bacon is not yet crisp, about 7 minutes. Set the bacon aside off the heat. In a medium bowl, whisk together the eggs, cream, ½ teaspoon each salt and pepper, and the nutmeg.

4 Pour the egg mixture into the cooled crust. Sprinkle the bacon evenly over the top. Bake the quiche until the top is golden but not browned, 50 minutes to 1 hour. Let cool slightly on a wire rack before serving.

Roast Chicken and Potatoes
Poulet Rôti

This simple, elegant method for roasting chicken (see photograph, page 134) gets an extra-rich savor from butter and a variety of herbs that steam in the interior of the chicken as it cooks, infusing the meat with flavor while keeping it moist. As excellent as it is hot out of the oven, the leftovers make for terrific picnic food. Be sure to use a chicken of high quality.

Delicious Little Sparrows

Spaetzle is a simple egg-and-flour pasta, an old Western European dish (the word means "little sparrows" in Swabian German) that in France is associated with Alsace, the northeast region that borders Germany. The cut's rough irregular shape allows sauces to cling easily to it, like the one in Rabbit Stew with Bacon and Dijon Mustard (page 138). To make enough to serve four people, bring a large pot of salted water to a rolling boil. Meanwhile, in a medium bowl, use a fork to combine 1½ cups all-purpose flour with a hefty pinch or two of salt. Gradually mix in 2 eggs and ½ cup water until a loose dough forms. Put the dough onto a moistened cutting board in a ¼ inch-thick layer, shaping it with your fingers into a rectangular shape. Using the edge of a knife, scrape long, thin strands, about ¼ inch thick, directly into the boiling water. The strands of dough cook quickly, in about a minute—they'll float to the surface when they're done. If necessary, cook them in batches, transferring them with a slotted spoon to a colander. Finally, heat a skillet over medium-high heat. Melt a good quantity of butter (at least half a stick), add the cooked spaetzle, working in batches if necessary, and sauté just until they're golden and ever-so-slightly crisp on the outside and wonderfully soft and warm on the inside. Serve the spaetzle immediately.

Rabbit Stew with Bacon and Dijon Mustard (page 138), served with homemade spaetzle (left).

Serves 4

> 1 whole small chicken, 4½ to 5 pounds
> 3 tablespoons unsalted butter, at room temperature
> 3 garlic cloves, well bruised and coarsely chopped
> ½ lemon, seeded
> Salt and freshly ground black pepper
> 10 fresh flat-leaf parsley sprigs
> 20 fresh or dried thyme sprigs (optional)
> 1½ pounds small fingerling or Yukon gold potatoes, unpeeled (about 5 cups)
> 2 tablespoons extra-virgin olive oil, plus more for the chicken

1 Preheat the oven to 400°F. Pat the chicken thoroughly dry with paper towels. Using your fingers, loosen the skin from the breast meat on both sides, being careful not to tear the skin. Slip most of the butter under the loosened skin, massaging it into the meat and pushing it down into the thigh joints. Spread a little of the remaining butter on the skin covering the breasts and thighs. Stuff about half of the garlic between the skin and the meat, spreading it evenly across the breast. Squeeze most of the juice from the lemon half over the outside of the chicken and reserve the partially spent lemon half. Sprinkle 1 teaspoon each salt and pepper evenly over the outside of the chicken, then season the cavity with ½ teaspoon salt and the remaining juice from the lemon half. Slip the spent lemon half into the cavity and then stuff the cavity with the parsley and thyme, if using.

2 Grease a roasting pan—it should be shallow and roomy enough to hold the chicken and potatoes—with the remaining butter. Place the chicken, breast side up, in the pan and put the potatoes around the bird. Drizzle the potatoes with the oil and sprinkle them generously with salt and pepper. Scatter the remaining garlic over the potatoes, then turn the potatoes to coat them evenly with the oil and seasonings. Drizzle a little oil on the chicken.

3 Roast the chicken for 45 minutes. Raise the oven temperature to 475°F and continue to roast, basting every 15 minutes with the pan juices, until the skin is deeply golden and an instant-read thermometer inserted into the thigh away from bone registers 165°F, about 1 hour longer (1¾ hours total cooking time more or less, depending on how well done you like your chicken). Alternatively, to test for doneness, pierce the thigh joint with a knife tip; the juices should run clear. The potatoes are ready when they can be easily pierced with a fork.

4 Transfer the chicken to a cutting board or platter, tent with aluminum foil, and let rest for 15 minutes before carving. Serve with the potatoes.

Rabbit Stew with Bacon and Dijon Mustard
Lapin aux Lardons et Moutarde

This Alsatian dish (see photograph, page 137) is the epitome of French country home cooking. Since no thickener is used, there are abundant savory, winey juices, so it's excellent served on a bed of wide, flat egg noodles or pappardelle. Yves Koerkel, a Paris-based artist who prepares a dish much like this regularly for his family, makes homemade spaetzle (page 136) to serve along with it.

Serves 4

> 2 tablespoons extra-virgin olive oil
> 7 ounces slab bacon, cut into lardons 2 inches long and ¼ inch wide and thick (about 1½ cups)
> 1 rabbit (see page 195), about 4½ pounds, cut into six pieces
> Salt and freshly ground black pepper
> 1 tablespoon unsalted butter
> 1 medium yellow onion, halved
> 1 tablespoon Dijon mustard
> 1 cup soft, smooth red wine (such as Merlot)
> 2 cups French Chicken Broth (page 188)

Bouquet garni (2 bay leaves, a few fresh or
dried thyme sprigs, a few fresh or dried
oregano sprigs)
1 pound medium cremini or button mushrooms,
thickly sliced lengthwise
Parsley leaves, chopped, for garnish
Cooked spaetzle (page 136) or wide, flat noodles,
for serving

1 In a 5-quart Dutch oven, heat the oil over
medium heat. Add the bacon and fry, stirring
occasionally, until just golden, about 7 minutes.
Using a slotted spoon, transfer the bacon to
a plate.

2 Season the rabbit pieces with ½ teaspoon
each salt and pepper. Add the butter to the
Dutch oven and allow it to melt into the bacon
fat. Working in batches, add the rabbit pieces
and onion halves and cook, turning as needed,
until the rabbit is golden on all sides, about 7
minutes. (If liquid starts to collect in the pot,
tilt the pot and scoop it out and discard it or the
rabbit won't brown properly.) As each batch is
ready, transfer it to a plate.

3 When all of the rabbit and the onion halves
are browned, return them to the pot along
with the reserved bacon and add the mustard
and wine and mix to incorporate. Raise the
heat to medium-high and bring the liquid to a
boil. The moment the mixture reaches a boil,
turn down the heat to medium-low and cook
uncovered at a gentle simmer (adjust the heat
as necessary and be vigilant that it does not
boil), stirring occasionally, until the wine has
reduced by about 90 percent and has been
mostly absorbed into the meat, about 30 minutes. Add the broth and bouquet garni, turn
down the heat to low, cover, and simmer, taking care never to let the liquid boil, until the
meat is tender, about 2 hours. (Note that when
the meat is ready, it will still be somewhat firm,
as rabbit, unlike chicken, does not generally
soften and fall off the bone.)

4 Add the mushrooms, re-cover, and cook
over low heat until they are fork-tender, 15 to
20 minutes. Garnish with the parsley and serve
hot with the spaetzle.

6

Tradition That Is Baked In

Breads and Pastries

In her home kitchen, Dorie Greenspan slices into a still-warm choux pastry. Page 140: Puff Pastry with Salt-Packed Anchovies (page 157).

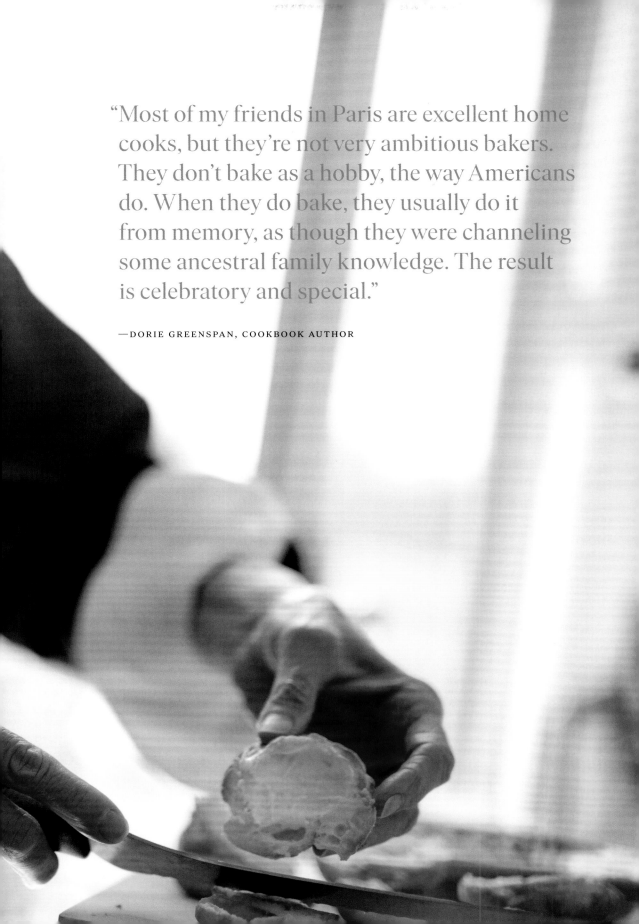

"Most of my friends in Paris are excellent home cooks, but they're not very ambitious bakers. They don't bake as a hobby, the way Americans do. When they do bake, they usually do it from memory, as though they were channeling some ancestral family knowledge. The result is celebratory and special."

—DORIE GREENSPAN, COOKBOOK AUTHOR

Here in the eighteenth arrondissement, it is just after seven o'clock in the morning, and a line of customers is already forming outside the sleek modern *boulangerie* on the corner. Inside, on the right side of the counter, are pastries based on the crispy-soft dough *pâte à choux*, such as éclairs—thin, four-inch-long batons usually filled with vanilla custard and topped with chocolate glaze. To the left of them are arrangements of pastries made of versions of the lavishly buttery *pâte feuilletée*, or puff pastry, dough: napoleons with their alternating layers of creamy custard and crisp pastry; a stack of glistening croissants recently out of the oven. The latter will most likely be consumed for breakfast along with a dollop of fruit preserves and a shot of espresso.

And then, behind the counter on tall shelves and lined up like soldiers standing at attention, is the bread. A best seller in this *boulangerie* is the *baguette de tradition*, which is also known as *baguette à l'ancienne*, hinting at the recipe's venerable roots. This is a hand-formed loaf, rough in appearance and made with a sourdough starter. It has a more rustic taste and texture than the world-famous *baguette ordinaire*, sometimes called *baguette parisienne*. The latter is leavened with yeast rather than starter, and it is such a crucial staple that government legislation dictates its exact composition.

Strict laws also govern the hours of operation for a *boulangerie*. Because this one is open for only a handful of hours, the counter service is cheery but brisk, which means you'd better step lively when it is your turn to order.

"Une tradition, s'il vous plaît," says a young man, rubbing sleep from his eyes. It is likely that he's a newlywed from the apartment complex next door on his usual morning jaunt to fill his wife's boulangerie order before he dashes off to work. The woman at the counter, elegant in a crisp blue smock, asks, "Do you want anything else?" He quickly settles on two *pains au chocolat*, croissants with a ribbon of dark chocolate baked in the center. They're still warm when she pops them into a paper bag.

All over Paris, the morning air is fragrant with the aroma of baking dough. Not far away from the *boulangerie*, a Syrian baker on the Rue du Faubourg du Temple is hard at work. His ovens have been blazing since dawn, and soon he will be flooded with eager customers lining up to buy his flatbread, for the baking traditions of North Africa and the Middle East are an integral part of the city's love affair with bread. For lunch on the go, all manner of people stop by his shop to buy his *lahmajun*, light, soft flatbread topped with spicy ground lamb and garnished with chopped parsley, a squeeze of lemon juice, and a pinch of ground Aleppo pepper. Although a relatively recent arrival to the streets of Paris, *lahmajun* has become a favorite in a city whose residents treat bread with a kind of religious reverence.

The Paris baking technique is a marriage of science and nature, systematized to reach a level of unparalleled precision, and it has been so for generations. And with three James Beard awards and six French food–themed cookbooks under her belt, Dorie Greenspan, a Brooklynite by birth, is arguably as well credentialed in matters concerning French baking as it's possible to be. This morning, Greenspan is baking in the kitchen of her garret apartment near the Saint-Germain-des-Prés métro station.

She and her husband, Michael, have lived in and out of Paris for years, but they've only recently moved to this address. She loves the apartment's narrow wraparound balcony, her face lighting up whenever her gaze catches its view of treetops and the Eiffel Tower. Right now the door to the balcony in her kitchen is open, and the sound of someone singing a melody from *La Traviata* wafts up from the sidewalk below: *"Libiamo, libiamo ne'lieti calici, che la belleza infiora!"* Setting out four eggs and a block of bittersweet chocolate to come to room temperature, Greenspan finds herself humming along with the stranger. Knowing that every oven has its idiosyncrasies, and not yet intimately acquainted with the one in this kitchen, she places an oven thermometer on its middle rack when she heats it.

Her project today is *pâte à choux* for a batch of classic profiteroles. The staple dough is shiny and elastic in its raw state, then develops an appealingly fissured surface during baking. Although the result is tender and delicate, the dough is relatively straight-forward to make, chiefly a question of adding and blending ingredients until a silken consistency is reached. The result she is aiming for are globe-like puffs of pastry, which she'll stuff with vanilla ice cream, drizzle with a warm chocolate sauce, then enjoy as a special treat with her husband.

The dough is ready to form. Since touching *pâte à choux* with one's fingers can cause immediate melting, Greenspan uses a scoop to place portions of it on a parchment paper–lined baking sheet. Then into the oven the baking sheet goes. A little bit later, while the picture-perfect golden pastry puffs are still warm, she uses a serrated knife to slice them not quite all the way through. Ice cream is spooned into each. Finally, over the filled puffs, she pours a stream of the cream-enriched chocolate sauce that she'd made earlier. She stands back to study her creation. The small crease in her brow reveals concern. Is there something about her profiteroles that could be improved upon? Was her new oven going to require a few more sessions to better understand its peculiarities? Her husband's contented smile upon encountering his first bite is all the confirmation needed: the profiteroles are perfect.

Bread on the Table

With its crackling amber crust, springy-chewy interior, and malty flavor, the baguette is a basic furnishing of the Parisian meal—as necessary as salt. The long, thin loaf—the word *baguette* means "wand"—was officially christened in Paris in the 1920s. After World War II, bakers started producing an additive-heavy baguette dough that could be industrially produced and frozen. In 1993, however, the government issued a "bread decree," establishing conditions for what would constitute a *baguette de tradition française*: among other things, it had to be free of additives, naturally fermented, and freshly made on the premises. Hence, the true baguette was restored to its glory. The types shown at right are common to nearly every *boulangerie*. The **campagne** ① sometimes has no diagonal cuts on the surface. The deeply golden **tradition** ② is the standard-bearer. The **ordinaire** or **Parisienne**, ③ with pretty slits on its top, is reliably excellent. The **grain** or **cereale** ④, a whole-wheat version, has a rustic flavor. Some prefer the roasted flavor of a *tradition* loaf that is baked until it is almost burnt, or **bien cuit** ⑤. A very thin baguette, or **ficelle** ⑥, has extra crunch. (For more information about baguettes, see page 188.)

① ② ③ ④ ⑤ ⑥

"When I first came to Paris years ago from Sweden, I fell under the spell of the city's baguettes. They were so crunchy, chewy, and sublime—nothing like I previously understood baguettes to be. I'm a doctor, so I was determined to crack the code. I went to baking school and worked in several traditional bakeries. I even considered changing careers. In the end, I didn't. But I learned that French breadmaking is not only a science. It is a form of magic."

—AXEL RODHE, PARIS-BASED PHYSICIAN

Puff Pastry with Salt-Packed Anchovies

Feuilleté d'Anchois

This is an unforgettably good meal: anchovies arranged on a layer of onion marmalade, baked on a crisp golden rectangle of puff pastry and then dusted with Parmesan cheese (see photographs, page 140). Homemade puff pastry will make this dish something to write home about, but a quality store-bought puff pastry can be substituted if necessary. Serve with a green salad and a refreshing white wine, such as Sancerre.

Serves 4

- About 17 salt-packed anchovies, or about 34 olive oil–packed anchovy fillets (see page 191)
- 1 cup whole milk (optional)
- Half batch French Puff Pastry (page 194) or 1¼ pounds thawed store-bought all-butter puff pastry, such as Dufour (see page 193)
- All-purpose flour, for the work surface
- 1 egg yolk, lightly beaten
- 2 tablespoons extra-virgin olive oil
- 1 medium yellow onion, sliced vertically into ¼-inch-thick slices
- Salt
- 2 tablespoons grated Parmesan cheese

1 If using salt-packed anchovies, combine the anchovies with the milk to cover and soak for 15 minutes to rid them of excessive saltiness. Pat them dry and fillet them as directed on page 191, discarding the heads and tails but leaving the skin intact. If using anchovy fillets packed in oil, drain them well and blot thoroughly with paper towels.

2 Preheat the oven to 375°F. If using store-bought pastry, unfold the sheets gently to avoid cracking (if the pastry is not pliable, let sit at room temperature until it is). Place the dough—homemade or store-bought—on a lightly floured surface and sprinkle a little flour on top of it. Gently roll into a rectangle about 13 by 9 inches and about ⅓ inch thick. Work swiftly so the dough doesn't warm up. Carefully transfer the dough to an 18 by 13-inch sheet pan. Brush the edges of the dough rather heavily with the egg yolk to make a "frame." Bake the pastry until it is about half cooked and the surface is just becoming golden, about 30 minutes.

3 Meanwhile, in a medium saucepan, heat the oil over low heat. Add the onion and cook, stirring occasionally, until the onion is beginning to caramelize—it should be just golden, no darker, 20 to 25 minutes.

4 When the pastry is ready, remove it from the oven and evenly spread the onion marmalade on top of it, staying inside the "frame" created by the egg wash. Arrange the anchovy fillets in neat rows on top of the marmalade. Return the pastry to the oven and bake until the pastry is fully cooked and the edges are deeply golden, about 30 minutes. Sprinkle the Parmesan evenly over the top and serve immediately.

Dorie Greenspan's Ice Cream–Filled Choux Pastries with Chocolate Sauce

Profiteroles

Dorie Greenspan is one of the greatest interpreters of French baking—and this is one of her finest recipes, a celebratory dessert made of tender puffs of *pâte à choux* dough filled with vanilla ice cream and drizzled with a warm homemade chocolate sauce. The cooked pastry puffs can, if packed in an airtight container, be frozen for up to 2 months, then crisped for a few minutes in a 350°F oven before filling and serving. The sauce can be refrigerated for up to a week, then reheated just before using. Using a stand mixer will help make a more reliable dough.

Dorie Greenspan's Ice Cream–Filled Choux Pastries with Chocolate Sauce.

Makes about 24 profiteroles

PUFFS

1 cup whole milk

½ cup water

½ cup (1 stick) unsalted butter, cut into
**   4 equal pieces**

1 tablespoon sugar

½ teaspoon salt

1 cup all-purpose flour

4 eggs, at room temperature

CHOCOLATE SAUCE

½ cup heavy cream

½ cup water

4 ounces bittersweet chocolate, chopped

Ice cream, for filling the puffs (vanilla
**   is traditional)**

1 Arrange an oven rack in the center of the oven and preheat it to 425°F. Line two sheet pans with parchment paper, waxed paper, or silicone baking mats. In a heavy medium saucepan, combine the milk, water, butter, sugar, and salt and bring to a boil over medium-high heat; immediately reduce the heat to medium. Add the flour and stir energetically with a wooden spoon or heavy heat-resistant spatula. The dough will soon come together in a ball, and a thin, light crust will form on the bottom of the pan.

2 Remove from the heat and transfer the dough to a stand mixer fitted with the paddle attachment. (This step can also be done with a large bowl and a handheld mixer.) With the mixer on medium speed, add the eggs, one at a time, beating after each addition until the egg is fully incorporated and the dough is very smooth and the consistency of toothpaste. Don't worry if the dough separates during the beating; it will come together by the time the last egg is incorporated. Once all of the eggs have been added, continue beating on medium speed until the dough is silky and soft, about 5 minutes.

3 While the dough is still warm, shape the puffs. You want about 1½ tablespoons of dough for each puff; use a rounded tablespoonful or

a medium-size ice cream scoop. Scoop out the dough onto the prepared sheet pans, spacing the puffs about 2 inches apart.

4 Place a sheet pan in the oven and immediately turn down the oven temperature to 375°F. Bake for 20 minutes, then open the oven door (which helps release any trapped steam) and rotate the pan. Continue to bake the puffs until they are golden brown, firm, and sound hollow when tapped on the bottom, 10 to 15 minutes. Transfer them to wire racks and let cool to room temperature. Repeat with the other sheet pan.

5 To make the chocolate sauce, in a heavy medium saucepan, stir together the cream, water, and chocolate and bring to a boil over medium-low heat, stirring constantly. Turn down the heat to low and continue stirring constantly. Simmer until the sauce thickens, 10 to 15 minutes. To test if it is ready, dip a metal spoon into the sauce, then draw your finger through the sauce on the back of the spoon; the track should remain clear. Remove from the heat and let cool for 10 minutes.

6 Using a serrated knife and a sawing motion, cut each puff in half horizontally. Add a scoop of ice cream to the bottom of each puff and replace the top. Arrange the filled puffs on a serving plates; allow 2 to 3 per person. Drizzle the warm chocolate sauce over the puffs and serve at once.

Puff Pastry with Strawberries and Vanilla Custard

Mille-Feuille aux Fraises

Berries and homemade custard nestled between layers of flaky puff pastry and presented with a strawberry sauce add up to a truly world-class dessert (see photograph, page 163). Use ripe, sweet, preferably small strawberries. Much of what makes this dish memorable rests on the quality of the pastry, so if you are not using homemade puff pastry, be sure your store-bought pastry is the best you can find.

Serves 4

STRAWBERRY SAUCE

1 cup medium strawberries (about 6 ounces), stemmed and cut in half

½ cup sugar

VANILLA CUSTARD

2⅓ cups whole milk

¼ teaspoon pure vanilla extract

1 whole egg

2 egg yolks

½ cup sugar

2 tablespoons cornstarch

Half batch French Puff Pastry (page 194) or 1¼ pounds thawed store-bought all-butter puff pastry, such as Dufour (see page 193)

All-purpose flour, for the work surface

½ to 1 cup small strawberries, hulled and thickly sliced if large or whole or halved if small

1 To make the sauce, place the strawberries and sugar in a small saucepan over medium-low heat. Cook the strawberries, stirring often, until they begin to soften. Mash them with the back of a spoon until you have a mushy, syrupy stew. Simmer gently, stirring occasionally, for 10 minutes. Remove the saucepan from the heat and strain the strawberries through a fine-mesh sieve into a bowl, pressing them with a spoon to extract as much syrup as possible. Set the syrup aside in a warm place.

2 To make the custard, in a small saucepan, heat the milk and the vanilla over low heat until small bubbles appear along the edge of the liquid. While the milk heats, in a medium bowl, whisk together the whole egg, egg yolks, and sugar until the sugar has dissolved. Whisk in the cornstarch until thoroughly incorporated. Remove the saucepan containing the milk from the heat, and slowly add about ½ cup of the hot milk to the egg mixture while whisking constantly. Pour the milk-egg mixture into the remaining warm milk, return the saucepan containing the milk to low heat, and bring to a gentle simmer while whisking continuously to avoid lumps. If any of the custard starts to stick to the sides of the pan, leave it there; don't scrape it off, as it won't reincorporate. Cook, stirring constantly, until a thick custard or pudding consistency is achieved, about 10 minutes. Remove from the heat and pour into a bowl. Cover with plastic wrap, pressing the wrap directly onto the surface of the custard to prevent a skin from forming, and let cool completely.

3 Preheat the oven to 375°F. If using store-bought pastry, unfold the sheets gently to avoid cracking (if the pastry is not pliable, let it sit for a few more minutes at room temperature). Place the dough—homemade or store-bought—on a lightly floured surface and sprinkle a little flour on top of it. Gently roll into a 13 by 9-inch rectangle about ⅓ inch thick. Work swiftly so the dough does not warm up.

4 Carefully transfer the dough to a sheet pan. Cut it lengthwise into three pieces of equal size. Arrange the pieces ½ inch apart on the pan. Bake until they become puffy and golden-brown, 30 to 40 minutes. Transfer the pastry pieces to wire racks until they are cool enough to handle.

5 Drizzle the strawberry sauce onto a serving plate; use a decorative circular pattern if you like. Place a whole piece of the pastry on top of the sauce. With a piping bag fitted with a small plain tip or with a spoon, pipe or spread about half of the custard onto the pastry. Top with a bit less than half of the strawberries. Top the strawberries with another piece of pastry, then top the pastry with the remaining custard. Arrange almost all of the remaining berries on the custard and then add the final layer of pastry. Scatter the remaining strawberries atop the pastry and alongside it. Serve immediately.

Syrian-Style Flatbread with Spicy Lamb Topping
Lahmajun

This thin flatbread topped with seasoned ground lamb and a bright-tasting garnish of

parsley and onions is a popular Parisian meal on the go, and makes for a satisfying appetizer, light meal, or picnic lunch. Turkish red pepper paste is made from mild peppers; look for it online or at shops selling Turkish or Middle Eastern foods (its Turkish name is *biber salçasi*). This recipe (see photograph, page 145) is adapted from one by Turkish-Australian chef and cookbook author Somer Sivrioglu.

Makes 4 flatbreads

FLATBREAD

1¾ cups plus 1 tablespoon all-purpose flour, sifted, plus more for the work surface

1 teaspoon salt

½ cup warm water, plus more if needed

TOPPING

1 Roma tomato, grated

3 tablespoons mild Turkish red pepper paste or tomato paste

2 garlic cloves, minced

¼ medium yellow onion, minced

1½ tablespoons minced fresh flat-leaf parsley

¼ teaspoon cayenne pepper

Generous pinch of ground cumin

Salt and freshly ground black pepper

3½ ounces ground lamb

HERB GARNISH

1 cup loosely packed fresh flat-leaf parsley leaves

1 teaspoon ground Aleppo pepper (optional)

½ small red onion, very thinly sliced horizontally

4 lemon wedges

1 Select a sheet pan, then cut four sheets of parchment paper that will cover the bottom of the pan. Set the parchment sheets aside. Place the sheet pan into the oven and preheat the oven to 550°F.

2 In a large bowl, whisk together the flour and salt, then make a well in the center. Slowly drizzle the warm water into the well and, using a wooden spoon, gradually stir the flour into the water until fully mixed and a rough mass forms. If the dough

is not forming, stir in 1 to 2 tablespoons more warm water. Knead the dough in the bowl until smooth and elastic, about 5 minutes. Transfer the dough to a lightly floured work surface. Divide the dough into four equal portions and shape each portion into a ball. Place the dough balls on a room-temperature sheet pan, cover with a clean, damp cloth, and set aside.

3 In a bowl, combine the tomato, pepper paste, garlic, onion, parsley, cayenne, cumin, and ¼ teaspoon each salt and pepper. Using a fork, mix well, then taste for salt and add more if needed. Add the lamb and mix well.

4 Have the four parchment sheets ready. On a lightly floured work surface, roll out one of the balls of dough into an oval about 12 inches long and 8 inches wide. Lightly dust one of the parchment sheets with flour and transfer the oval to it. Repeat with the remaining dough balls, adding each oval to a flour-dusted parchment sheet.

5 Keeping each rolled oval on its sheet of parchment, spoon about 3½ tablespoons of the topping onto each one. Using your fingers or a spoon, spread it very thinly to reach the edges of the dough. Carefully remove the heated sheet pan from the oven, lift a flatbread-topped parchment sheet onto the hot pan, and return the pan to the oven. Bake until the edges of the dough are just beginning to pick up golden spots and the topping is cooked, about 5 minutes; the bread should be pliant, not crisp. Transfer the flatbread to a wire rack and repeat with the remaining flatbreads.

6 In a small bowl, mix together the parsley, Aleppo pepper (if using), and onion. Serve the flatbreads warm or at room temperature. Just before serving, top the middle of each flatbread with one-fourth of the herb garnish; serve with lemon wedges for squeezing on top. To eat, invite each diner to roll up a flatbread as if it were a burrito.

Home cook Deborah Zago holds a plate of her Real French Toast (page 162).

Real French Toast

Pain Perdu

When prepared in this way, French toast (see photograph, page 160) is like a warm bread pudding: crisp and golden outside with a custardy interior and just a little sweet. In France, it is traditionally served as a dessert. Eat it plain or top to your taste with maple syrup or fruit preserves—or a dusting of confectioners' sugar, as is traditional.

Serves 4
- ⅓ **cup whole milk**
- ⅓ **cup heavy cream**
- **4 eggs**
- **2 to 3 tablespoons granulated sugar**
- **Salt**
- **2 tablespoons unsalted butter, plus more as needed for cooking and serving**
- **1 day-old baguette or ½ loaf crusty Italian-style bread (about 7 ounces), cut into ¾-inch-thick slices (about 16 slices)**
- **Fruit preserves, warm maple syrup, or confectioners' sugar, for serving**

1 Preheat the oven to its lowest setting. In a bowl, whisk together the milk, cream, eggs, granulated sugar, and a pinch of salt until fully blended. Heat a 12-inch skillet over medium-low heat. Add 1 tablespoon of the butter and allow it to melt. (Keep the butter from browning throughout the cooking process by adjusting the heat as necessary.) Soak a slice of bread in the egg-milk mixture until the mixture reaches the center and add it to the pan; repeat with as many more bread slices as will comfortably fit. Cook 2 to 3 minutes on each side, until both sides are golden. Transfer to a heatproof plate and keep warm in the oven. Melt the remaining 1 tablespoon butter in the skillet and continue to soak and cook the remaining slices, adding butter as needed and keeping the cooked slices warm in the oven.

2 Serve topped with butter and the topping of your choice.

Parisian Ham Sandwiches, Two Ways

Jambon-beurre (see photograph, page 148, top), the reigning street food of Paris, consists of Paris-style ham between two pieces of baguette spread with a good deal of butter. The variation adds goat cheese and a garlicky *pistou*.

Classic Parisian Ham and Butter Sandwich

Jambon-Beurre
Serves 1
- ½ **baguette**
- **3 tablespoons unsalted butter, at room temperature**
- **2 slices Paris-style ham (see page 193)**

Slice the baguette in half horizontally. Evenly spread the butter on both cut sides before adding the ham. Serve.

Chez Aline's Ham, Chèvre, and Pesto Baguette Sandwich

Baguette de Jambon avec Pistou
Serves 1
- **1 cup loosely packed fresh basil leaves**
- **1 cup loosely packed fresh flat-leaf parsley leaves**
- **2 garlic cloves, bruised**
- ⅓ **cup grated Parmesan cheese**
- ½ **cup hazelnuts or almonds**
- ½ **cup extra-virgin olive oil**
- **Salt and freshly ground black pepper (optional)**
- ½ **baguette**
- **About 2 ounces chèvre (see page 33)**
- **2 slices Paris-style ham (see page 193)**

1 In a blender, combine the basil, parsley, garlic, Parmesan, hazelnuts, and oil and blend until a coarse paste forms. Season to taste with salt and pepper (if using).

2 Slice the baguette in half horizontally. Slather each cut side with 2 tablespoons of the pesto, then spread the chèvre on both cut sides, add the ham, and serve.

Puff Pastry with Strawberries and Vanilla Custard (page 158).

7

Sugar,
Butter,
Flair,
Precision

Desserts

Having purchased some of the finest chocolate that money can buy, a customer departs the internationally acclaimed chocolatier Pierre Hermé. Page 164: Marshmallows (page 176).

*Whimsical and delicious,
Parisian Black-and-White
Cookies (page 177) tempt
adults and children alike.*

I n the landscaped courtyard of the
École Grégoire-Ferrandi, arguably
the world's most important cooking
school, daffodils sway on their stalks
and the trees are budding. But hardly
any of the hundreds of pupils scur-
rying to class notice. Soon after its inception
in 1932, Ferrandi, as it is commonly known,
became the model for culinary institutes
across the globe, and studying here in one of
the many professional courses they offer is
serious business.

Today, inside a class on desserts, Michelle
Kusuma, a thoughtful student in her twenties,
is melting chocolate in a double boiler. She
shoots a glance at her classmates, hoping for
reassurance that she is getting the consistency
exactly right for ganache. Kusuma can't catch
anyone's eye, though, because everyone else
is moving around with similar focus and
intent. The room is like an immaculate hive
of busy, white-clad bees, the pupils in their
crisp uniforms and toques wholly absorbed in
their tasks.

Now the students are to put their chocolate aside to cool and to observe as the
instructor gives a demonstration. Kusuma
sets her whisk down and gathers with the
others. They are the picture of attentiveness
as he pours fruit reduction into a cake mold.
Murmurs of admiration rise as, with the del-
icacy of a surgeon, he lifts an impossibly thin
layer of chocolate cake and sets it into the

mold without a single crack appearing on its
surface. He drizzles more fruit reduction in,
and a hush descends as Kusuma and her fellow
pupils take notes.

Meanwhile, another culinary lesson
on dessert is unfolding in the apartment of
Frédéric Ramade, the filmmaker friend of
Bénédict Beaugé. Ramade has a wide circle
of acquaintances, and right now, Kaï Robert,
the eighteen-year-old son of a colleague, is
texting him for instructions on making *soufflé
au Grand Marnier*. The egg whites have formed
soft peaks, but he forgot the pinch of salt—has
he ruined them? Ramade, in his chic white
apron, sets down a platter of appetizers to text
the youth a message of encouragement: "Not
at all. You add the salt after the peaks form.
You're doing great!"

It's not an opportune moment for a tuto-
rial, but Ramade is always obliging if it means
facilitating someone's enjoyment of good food.
That explains why, despite the minuscule
dimensions of his kitchen, there are eight
dinner guests crowded into his flat for Sunday
lunch this afternoon. All of them are also fans
of gastronomy and, having finished the *apéro*
and the first course, they are excited to see
the main dish, a roast. His phone chimes with
another anxious query from Robert. Ramade
taps back a reply ("It will become golden on
top after it rises"), then returns to his guests,
smiling. "Pardon me," he says, "dessert waits
for no man."

There are projects to discuss, a smattering of political opinions to air, a soupçon of film-industry gossip to confide over the cheese course. Robert reports via text that he has produced a successful soufflé, and Ramade places slices of *tarte à la rhubarbe*, a rustic rhubarb tart, onto china plates.

"Frédéric, this is excellent," says one of Ramade's smartly dressed guests. The crumbly, buttery crust has a sweet, nutty flavor that complements the sourness of the rhubarb. "The secret is a dusting of almond flour," Ramade tells her.

"I need this recipe," says another guest. Ramade says he would be pleased to share it, adding that it can also be made with peaches or plums.

The cake being taught in the classrooms of Ferrandi; the *soufflé au Grand Marnier* that Kaï Robert has made, fragrant with orange zest and citrus liqueur; the plenitude of fruit tarts found at every neighborhood *boulangerie*, as well as at Frédéric Ramade's lunch table—these are but three of the city's celebrated desserts. Parisian cookies are equally spectacular. Indeed, if Paris cannot claim the title of cookie capital of the world, it is surely a major contender. Take the classic treat *sablées de Paris*, shortbread-like in texture, with a whimsical design of alternating plain and chocolate layers, or the thin almond snaps known as *tuiles aux amandes*. Or raspberry-hazelnut butter cookies, a pretty pink wafer infused with homemade raspberry syrup. Marshmallows, with cheerful colors to match their many flavors, are another celebrated sweet.

Desserts here can be taken to baroque extremes, such as *île flottante*, "islands" of poached meringue drizzled with caramel syrup and set "afloat" on a pool of warm vanilla sauce. But they don't have to be flamboyant to be good. Real French toast, in which slices of baguette are soaked in cream and eggs and then sautéed in butter until golden, comforts with just the right amount of sweetness. And almost any bistro offers *crème brûlée*, a cool and creamy custard with a glassine crust achieved by applying a flame directly to the top. Cracking the surface of a *crème brûlée* with a spoon is surely one of the most satisfying possible ways to end a meal.

Pastry students at the École Grégoire-Ferrandi, one of the world's most important culinary schools, rapt in learning.

Home-Style Rhubarb Tart

Tarte à la Rhubarbe

Frédéric Ramade, from whose recipe this one is adapted (see photograph, page ii), bills his version as *tarte à la rhubarbe de ma mère revisitée* ("my mother's rhubarb tart revisited"). Nestled between the rhubarb and the crumbly crust is a layer of almond flour, which adds a nutty flavor and absorbs the small amount of liquid released during baking. The crust is a *pâte sablée*, a shortbread-style dough. If rhubarb isn't in season, you can substitute 1 pound small apricots or plums, halved and pitted, combined with ¼ cup sugar; no need to macerate them overnight, as with the rhubarb. Sprinkle with the almond flour and cook the tart until the fruit is fork-tender, about 55 minutes, omitting the drizzle of syrup (but not the lemon zest) at the end.

Serves 6 to 8

> 5 or 6 medium rhubarb stalks, leaves removed, ends trimmed, and cut into ½-inch pieces, or 1 pound frozen sliced rhubarb, thawed (about 3 cups)
> 4 tablespoons sugar
> 1 batch Shortbread-Style Pastry Dough (page 194)
> ¾ cup almond flour
> Finely grated zest of 1 lemon

1 The day before you assemble the tart, in a medium bowl, toss the rhubarb with 3 tablespoons of the sugar, coating evenly. Cover and let macerate in the refrigerator overnight, stirring occasionally.

2 The day you assemble the tart, remove the pastry from the refrigerator and let it sit at room temperature for 30 minutes. It should be pliable but still cool to the touch. Have ready an 11-inch tart pan with a removable bottom and two large sheets of parchment or waxed paper. When the dough is ready, unwrap it and place it between the two sheets of parchment. Using quick, decisive strokes, roll out the dough from the center outward with a rolling pin, rotating the dough a quarter turn after every couple of passes, until you have a round 13 inches in diameter and ¼ inch thick. Remove the top parchment sheet and invert the dough into the tart pan. Carefully peel away the second sheet, then gently press the dough onto the bottom and up the sides of the pan; trim the excess dough and discard. Chill the tart shell in the refrigerator for 30 minutes. Prick the bottom of the crust about twenty times with the tines of a fork.

3 Strain the liquid from the rhubarb into a saucepan. Add the remaining 1 tablespoon sugar to the saucepan, place over low heat, and simmer gently, stirring often, until the liquid has reduced to a thick syrup, about 10 minutes. Remove from the heat and let cool.

4 Preheat the oven to 375°F. Remove the chilled tart shell from the refrigerator. Spread the almond flour in an even layer on the bottom of the crust. Arrange the rhubarb pieces in concentric rings on top of the almond flour, packing them tightly. Sprinkle the lemon zest evenly over the top.

5 Bake the tart until the rhubarb is fork-tender and bubbling and the crust is golden and has pulled away slightly from the pan sides, 50 minutes to 1 hour. Transfer to a wire rack and let cool.

6 Drizzle the rhubarb syrup over the cooled tart; sprinkle lemon zest on top. Place the tart pan atop a small overturned bowl and gently slide the pan sides down away from the tart. Transfer the tart to a serving plate, carefully removing the bottom of the tart pan, and serve.

Marshmallows

Guimauves

Marshmallows have a history dating back to ancient Egypt, but it was the confectioners of 1800s Paris who perfected them. By flavoring them with extracts and using corresponding food colorings to tint them, you can create a range of tastes and hues as shown in the photograph on page 164; you can divide a batch to make more than one flavor and color. Note that you'll need a candy thermometer and a stand mixer to make this recipe.

Makes 24 marshmallows
   1 cup water
   3 envelopes (¼ ounce each) unflavored gelatin (about 7½ teaspoons total)
   1½ cups granulated sugar
   1 cup light corn syrup
   1 teaspoon alcohol-based fruit, herb, or nut extract (such as raspberry, almond, mint, lemon, or vanilla)
   12 drops red food coloring or coloring of choice
   Salt
   2 tablespoons confectioners' sugar
   2 tablespoons cornstarch
   Canola oil, for oiling the baking dish and spatula

1 Pour ½ cup of the water into the bowl of a stand mixer. Sprinkle the gelatin evenly over the water, stir, and let stand for 5 to 10 minutes. Have the whisk attachment ready.

2 In a small saucepan, combine the remaining ½ cup water, the granulated sugar, corn syrup, extract, food coloring, and a pinch of salt. Place the saucepan over medium-high heat, cover, and cook for 4 minutes. Uncover the saucepan, clip a candy thermometer onto the side of the pan, and cook until the mixture registers 240°F (soft-ball stage), about 7 minutes; stirring the liquid is unnecessary. Immediately remove from the heat.

3 Fit the mixer with the whisk attachment. Turn on the mixer to low speed and very slowly pour the sugar syrup down the side of the bowl into the gelatin mixture, being careful not to make contact with the whisk attachment. Increase the speed to high and whip until the mixture becomes very thick and glossy—it will resemble a sticky, shiny meringue—and has cooled to lukewarm, 12 to 15 minutes.

4 In a small bowl, stir together the confectioners' sugar and cornstarch. Lightly oil a 13 by 9-inch baking dish. Lightly dust the bottom and sides of the oiled dish with some of the sugar-cornstarch mixture, tapping out the excess back into the bowl.

5 When the mixture is lukewarm, have ready a lightly oiled rubber spatula. Transfer the mixture to the prepared baking dish (the mixture will be quite sticky) and spread it evenly in the dish with the spatula, smoothing the top. Using a small fine-mesh sieve, lightly dust the surface with some of the sugar-cornstarch mixture; reserve the remaining sugar-cornstarch mixture for later use. Cover the dish with a clean, dry kitchen towel (don't let it come in contact with the surface of the marshmallows) and let rest at room temperature for at least 4 hours or up to overnight, allowing the marshmallow mixture to stiffen.

6 Turn the marshmallow slab out onto a cutting board. Using a sharp knife dusted with some of the remaining sugar-cornstarch mixture, cut the slab into roughly 2-inch squares. Lightly dust all sides of each marshmallow with the remaining sugar-cornstarch mixture, mixing up more sugar and cornstarch if needed. Store marshmallows in an airtight container at room temperature for up to 2 weeks.

Parisian Black-and-White Cookies
Sablées de Paris

Sablé, literally "sand," here refers to a specific texture: pleasantly rough-textured and flaky with a bit of crispness. These cookies (see photograph, page 168), with their charming design of alternating plain and chocolate layers, employ a modified *sablée* dough as a base. Be sure to refrigerate the dough overnight.

Makes about 40 cookies
   PLAIN DOUGH
   ½ cup (1 stick) unsalted butter, at room temperature

Crème Brûlée (page 183), as served at Bouillon Chartier, is a much-adored dessert.

⅓ cup sugar

Salt

1 egg yolk, at room temperature

1 cup all-purpose flour, plus more for the
   work surface

CHOCOLATE DOUGH

5 tablespoons unsalted butter, at
   room temperature

1 ounce dark baking chocolate, melted and
   cooled to room temperature

⅓ cup sugar

Salt

1 egg yolk, at room temperature

¾ cup all-purpose flour

¼ cup unsweetened Dutch-processed cocoa
   powder

1 To make the plain dough, in a medium bowl, using a handheld mixer, beat the butter on medium speed until very creamy and smooth. Add the sugar and a pinch of salt and beat until fully combined, about 1 minute. On low speed, add the egg yolk and beat until blended. Turn off the mixer, add the flour, and, using a rubber spatula, mix until barely combined. Return the mixer to its lowest speed and beat until all of the flour is incorporated, about 1 minute. Take care not to overwork the dough, which should be clumpy and soft.

2 Working on a lightly floured surface, divide the plain dough into three equal portions. Press together two portions and, using your palms, roll the dough into a smooth cylinder about 8 inches long and 1¼ inches in diameter. Wrap the cylinder tightly in plastic wrap. Roll the third dough portion into a ball and wrap in plastic wrap. Refrigerate both shapes for 2 hours.

3 To make the chocolate dough, in a medium bowl, using the handheld mixer, beat together the butter and chocolate on medium speed until creamy and smooth. Add the sugar and a pinch of salt and beat until fully combined, about 1 minute. On low speed, add the egg yolk and beat until well blended. Turn off the mixer, add the flour and cocoa powder, and, using a rubber

spatula, mix until barely combined. Return the mixer to its lowest speed and beat until all of the flour and cocoa powder are incorporated, about 1 minute. Take care not to overwork the dough, which should be clumpy and soft.

4 Working on the lightly floured surface, divide the chocolate dough into three equal portions. Press together two portions and, using your palms, roll the dough into a smooth cylinder about 8 inches long and 1¼ inches in diameter. Wrap the cylinder very tightly in plastic wrap. Roll the third dough portion into a ball and wrap in plastic wrap. Refrigerate both shapes for 2 hours.

5 To make the cookies, unwrap the plain and chocolate refrigerated dough balls. On a lightly floured surface, roll out each ball into a smooth-edged rectangle about 4 inches wide and 8 inches long. Place the plain dough rectangle facing you horizontally. Unwrap the chocolate dough cylinder and place it atop the plain dough rectangle, flush with its upper edge. Roll the plain dough around the chocolate cylinder in the manner of a jelly roll. Using your fingers, smooth the seam. Now lay the plain dough cylinder on top of the chocolate rectangle the same way, then repeat the rolling and smoothing process. You will now have two cylinders: one chocolate outside and plain inside, and one plain outside and chocolate inside. Wrap each one with plastic wrap and refrigerate for 3 hours or overnight.

6 When the dough is sufficiently chilled, preheat the oven to 375°F. Have a sheet pan ready; there's no need to butter it or line it with parchment paper. Unwrap one of the cylinders and, using a sharp knife, cut it into slices about ⅛ to ¼ inch thick. Arrange the slices on the sheet pan, spacing them about 1½ inches apart. Bake the cookies until no longer raw and very lightly browned on the bottom, 12 to 15 minutes. Transfer to a wire rack and let cool completely. Repeat with the remaining cylinder, letting the sheet pan cool to the touch before baking the next batch. Store the cookies in an airtight container at room temperature for up to a few days.

Grand Marnier Soufflé
Soufflé au Grand Marnier

A good soufflé is all about the fluffy consistency it gets from beaten egg whites. This version (see photograph, page 171) has the sunny taste of Grand Marnier liqueur and orange zest. Like most dishes in the French canon, a soufflé takes some time to master, but don't be daunted. It isn't as difficult to prepare as legend would have it.

Serves 6

  5 egg yolks
  2 tablespoons unsalted butter, plus more
    for greasing the mold
  2 tablespoons all-purpose flour
  1 cup heavy cream
  ⅓ cup sugar, plus more for dusting the mold
  1½ teaspoons finely grated orange zest
    (from about 2 oranges)
  ¼ cup Grand Marnier
  6 egg whites, at room temperature
  ½ teaspoon cream of tartar
  Salt

1 Preheat the oven to 375°F. Butter a 10-inch soufflé dish and then dust with sugar, tapping out the excess.

2 In a large nonreactive bowl, whisk the egg yolks until blended. In a medium saucepan, melt the butter over medium heat. Add the flour, stir constantly until fully integrated, and then cook, stirring constantly, for 1 minute. Remove from the heat, add the cream, sugar, and orange zest, and whisk until incorporated. Return the pan to medium heat and whisk continuously just until the mixture begins to boil. Remove from the heat and, continuously whisking, slowly pour the hot cream mixture into the egg yolks until fully incorporated. Whisk in the Grand Marnier and set aside.

3 In a separate large bowl, using a handheld mixer, beat the egg whites on high speed until they form soft peaks. Add the cream of tartar and a pinch of salt and beat until hard peaks form, about 5 minutes.

4 Using a rubber spatula, scoop half of the egg whites into the cream-yolk mixture and then fold them in (gently, to retain the air bubbles). Scoop the remaining egg whites into the same cream-yolk mixture and fold them in gently just until no white streaks remain. Pour the mixture into the prepared soufflé dish and gently use the spatula to make it flat and even on top.

5 Bake the soufflé until it rises and the top is golden, about 50 minutes. To test if it is ready, insert a wooden skewer on the diagonal to the bottom of the dish; it should come out clean or just very lightly moist. Serve immediately.

Raspberry-Hazelnut Butter Cookies
Palets à la Framboise

These delightful fuchsia-colored treats (see photograph, page 172), of a type found at La Grande Épicerie de Paris, the city's finest ingredients emporium, are thin, crispy-soft, and infused with raspberry syrup.

Makes about 24 cookies

  1½ cups all-purpose flour
  1½ teaspoons baking powder
  ¼ teaspoon salt
  ½ cup (1 stick) plus 2 tablespoons unsalted
    butter, at room temperature
  ½ cup sugar
  1 egg
  2½ tablespoons raspberry syrup
    (such as Torani or Monin)
  Scant ¼ teaspoon red food coloring
  1 drop blue food coloring
  ½ teaspoon finely grated lemon zest
  ¼ cup finely chopped skinless hazelnuts

1 In a medium bowl, whisk together the flour, baking powder, and salt. In a large bowl, using a handheld mixer, beat together the butter and sugar on medium-high speed until light and fluffy, about 3 minutes. Add the egg, raspberry

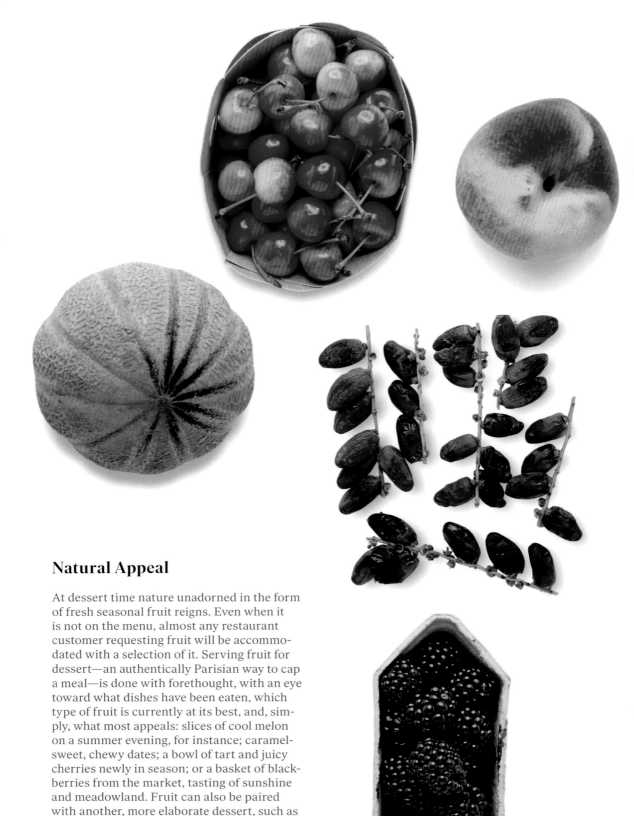

Natural Appeal

At dessert time nature unadorned in the form of fresh seasonal fruit reigns. Even when it is not on the menu, almost any restaurant customer requesting fruit will be accommodated with a selection of it. Serving fruit for dessert—an authentically Parisian way to cap a meal—is done with forethought, with an eye toward what dishes have been eaten, which type of fruit is currently at its best, and, simply, what most appeals: slices of cool melon on a summer evening, for instance; caramel-sweet, chewy dates; a bowl of tart and juicy cherries newly in season; or a basket of blackberries from the market, tasting of sunshine and meadowland. Fruit can also be paired with another, more elaborate dessert, such as a soft, perfectly ripe, and sweet peach alongside, say, *crème brûlée*.

syrup, both food colorings, lemon zest, and hazelnuts and beat until well combined. On low speed, gradually add the flour mixture and beat just until fully incorporated. The dough will be tacky.

2 Lay a sheet of plastic wrap on a work surface. Divide the dough in half and transfer half to the center of the plastic wrap. With your hands, shape the dough into a smooth cylinder 1½ inches in diameter and flatten both ends. (The dough will feel rather soft at this point.) Wrap the cylinder in the plastic wrap, sealing well. Repeat with a second piece of plastic wrap and the remaining dough. Refrigerate the cylinders for at least 2 hours or up to overnight.

3 Preheat the oven to 375°F. Line a large sheet pan with parchment paper, waxed paper, a silicone mat, or butter the pan. Unwrap a dough cylinder and, using a sharp knife, cut into slices ⅛ to ¼ inch thick. As the slices are cut, arrange them on the prepared pan, spacing them about 2 inches apart. Repeat with the remaining cylinder. You may need to manipulate the edges of each slice to create round, smooth-edged cookies.

4 Bake the cookies until the edges are lightly golden, about 15 minutes. Transfer to a wire rack and let cool for at least 20 minutes before serving—if you can wait that long. Store any leftovers in an airtight container at room temperature for up to a few days.

Crispy Almond Cookies
Tuiles aux Amandes

These delicate butter cookies (see photograph, page 173) have a crunchy snap and a nutty flavor. A terrific all-purpose cookie, they make an especially fine accompaniment to ice cream.

Makes 24 cookies

2 egg whites, at room temperature
⅓ cup plus 1 tablespoon sugar
Salt
¼ teaspoon pure almond extract
¼ teaspoon pure vanilla extract
½ cup all-purpose flour, sifted
5 tablespoons unsalted butter, melted and cooled to room temperature
½ cup sliced almonds

1 Preheat the oven to 375°F. Line a large sheet pan with parchment paper, waxed paper, or a silicone mat.

2 In a medium bowl, whisk together the egg whites, sugar, a pinch of salt, and both extracts until the sugar dissolves and the mixture is foamy. Gradually whisk in the flour until the mixture is smooth. Add the melted butter and mix just until blended.

3 Spoon about 1½ teaspoons of the batter onto the prepared pan and, using the back of a spoon, spread it into a thin round about 2½ inches in diameter. Repeat with the remaining batter, spacing the cookies about 3 inches apart. (You may need to press firmly with the back of the spoon to make circular shapes if the dough stiffens.) Evenly sprinkle the top of each cookie with a generous pinch of the almonds.

4 Bake until the cookies' centers are pale gold and their edges are golden brown, 8 to 10 minutes. Carefully transfer them to a cooling rack and let cool completely so they crisp up before serving. Store in an airtight container at room temperature for up to a few days.

Crème Brûlée

The de rigueur bistro dessert (see photograph, page 178), this simple cream-and-egg pudding is made sublime by the interplay of a warm, crunchy caramelized crust that contrasts with the creamy, cool custard below. You can serve the *crème* minus the brittle topping, either still warm from the oven or chilled, but it's traditional to apply a flame to the surface to achieve the crisp top.

Serves 6

    6 egg yolks

    ¼ cup sugar, plus 3 tablespoons for the topping

    2 cups heavy cream

1 Preheat the oven to 300°F. Have ready six ½-cup ramekins and a baking pan that is at least as deep as the ramekins and is large enough to accommodate them without crowding.

2 In a medium bowl, whisk together the egg yolks and sugar until the sugar dissolves. In a small saucepan, heat the cream over medium-low heat, stirring constantly with a heat-resistant spatula to ensure it is not sticking to the pan bottom, until small bubbles appear along the edge of the liquid, about 3 minutes. Remove the cream from the heat. While whisking continuously, gradually add the hot cream in a thin stream to the egg yolks until fully blended.

3 Strain the cream–egg yolk mixture through a fine-mesh sieve into a quart-size liquid measuring cup or a pitcher (to make filling the ramekins easier), then divide it evenly among the ramekins. Place the ramekins in the baking pan and add water to the pan to reach halfway up the sides of the ramekins. Carefully transfer the baking pan to the oven and bake until the custards are set at the edges and quiver slightly in the center when the ramekins are gently nudged, 45 to 50 minutes. To test, insert a small spoon into the center of a ramekin; the custard should be thick enough to coat the back of the spoon. Draw your finger through the sauce on the back of the spoon; the track should remain clear. If not, cook for a bit longer.

4 Remove the baking pan from the oven, then carefully transfer the ramekins to a wire rack and let cool to room temperature. Cover each ramekin with plastic wrap and refrigerate for at least 2 hours or, preferably, overnight (or up to 2 days).

"Floating Islands" with Caramel and Vanilla Sauce.

5 Just before serving, evenly sprinkle 1½ teaspoons of the sugar over the top of a custard, rotating the custard as you sprinkle to ensure even distribution. Repeat with the remaining sugar and custards. Holding the flame of a kitchen torch about 2 inches above the custard, move the flame over the surface in a circular motion. The sugar will melt and bead, then solidify into a crust. Continue to heat the surface until it has turned a caramel color, 1 to 2 minutes longer. (Keep in mind that the darker the crust gets, the more bitter it will taste.) Repeat with the remaining custards, then serve at once.

"Floating Islands" with Caramel and Vanilla Sauce

Île Flottante

A true showstopper, *île flottante* is springy clouds of poached meringue "floating" on a silky pool of vanilla sauce and drizzled with caramel syrup.

Serves 6

    VANILLA SAUCE

    2⅓ cups whole milk

    1 vanilla bean, or ½ teaspoon pure vanilla extract

    6 egg yolks

    ⅔ cup sugar

    CARAMEL SYRUP

    ½ cup sugar

    2 tablespoons plus ⅓ cup water

    MERINGUE

    6 egg whites, at room temperature

    2 tablespoons sugar

    1 cup milk

1 First, make the vanilla sauce. Pour the milk into a medium saucepan. If using a vanilla bean, split the pod in half lengthwise with a knife, then, using the tip of the knife, scrape out the seeds and add them and the pod to the milk. If using vanilla extract, add it now. Place the saucepan over medium heat and bring to a simmer, stirring often and adjusting the heat as necessary to prevent the milk from boiling, about 5 minutes. While the milk heats, in a medium bowl, whisk the egg yolks with the sugar until the sugar dissolves and the mixture is fluffy and lighter in color.

2 Remove the milk from the heat and discard the vanilla bean pods (if used). Slowly add about one-third of the hot milk to the egg yolks, whisking continuously until fully blended. Add the egg yolk mixture to the saucepan, place over medium-low heat, and cook, stirring constantly with a wooden spoon and never allowing the mixture to boil, until the mixture is thick enough to coat the back of a spoon, 5 to 10 minutes. Draw your finger through the sauce on the back of the spoon; the track should remain clear. If any of the custard starts to stick to the sides of the pan as you cook, leave it there; don't try to scrape it off. Remove from the heat and transfer the sauce to a bowl. Cover with plastic wrap, pressing the wrap directly against the surface to prevent a skin from forming, and set aside.

3 To make the caramel syrup, in a small saucepan, combine the sugar and 2 tablespoons of the water and place over medium-high heat. Tilting the pan in a circular motion, cook until the sugar has combined with the water and begins to melt. Do not stir with a spoon, which could cause crystallization; instead, continue to move the pan in a circular motion, making sure not to let the liquid boil, until the sugar has dissolved. The liquid will then darken to a golden brown color, which will take about 4 minutes. Remove the pan from the heat, add the remaining ⅓ cup water, and immediately stir with a spoon until incorporated—the risk of crystallization has subsided. If lumps of crystallized sugar appear, return the pan to low heat and stir until they dissolve. Set aside.

4 To make the meringue, in a large bowl, using a handheld mixer, beat the egg whites until soft peaks form. Continuously beating, sprinkle in the sugar, a tablespoon or so at a time, gradually increasing the speed to high. When all of the

sugar has been added, keep beating until stiff, glossy peaks form, 8 to 10 minutes.

5 Have ready a plate lined with a clean, dry cloth. Pour the milk into a 12-inch skillet, then add water as needed for the liquid to reach 1½ inches up the sides of the pan. Place the skillet over the lowest heat setting and heat the liquid until it is warm but not simmering and small bubbles are forming around the edge of the pan. Using a standard-size metal kitchen spoon, scoop out meringue roughly the size of a grapefruit (if you wish to create a more refined-looking meringue, you can smooth out the sides with a spoon) and transfer it to the skillet. Add more meringue "islands" to the pan the same way, being careful not to crowd them. Let cook undisturbed for 2 minutes, then, using two spoons, gently flip them and cook for another 2 minutes. The meringues should be firm. Using a slotted spoon, transfer the meringues to the cloth-lined plate to absorb any liquid. Repeat with the remaining meringue and set aside.

6 If serving on individual plates, pour about ⅓ cup of the vanilla sauce onto each plate; if using a single platter, pour all of the sauce into a large, deep platter. Either way, place the meringues on top of the sauce, allowing one or two per person if making individual servings. Drizzle about 1 tablespoon of the caramel syrup over each meringue. Serve at once.

8

Paris
Référence

General Notes on Ingredients

Because much of the cooking done in the United States has its roots in the culinary traditions of Western Europe in general and France in particular, many of the ingredients used in these recipes are probably already familiar to you. From crème fraîche to Dijon mustard, myriad French-produced or French-style ingredients have found themselves at home on North American market shelves. However, to prepare food that tastes authentically Parisian, you'll need to use not only the specific ingredients called for but also the best-quality ingredients you can find. Your first choices for produce and dairy should be, for the sake of freshness and flavor, farmers' markets, farm stands, and natural-foods outlets, such as your local food co-op. If you live in a place with a good butcher, fishmonger, cheese shop, or baker, become friendly with the people who work there and familiarize yourself with the foods they sell. Another option is a grocer that carries a wide array of organic and specialty products, such as Whole Foods or Wegmans. However, if you shop with discernment

at even an ordinary chain supermarket, you should be able to locate excellent renditions of virtually every ingredient called for in this book. For harder-to-find foods, such as Paris-style ham (see page 193), a little research will lead you to a wealth of reputable online retailers.

Bacon An essential ingredient of many French dishes is the lardon, a matchstick-size strip of salt-cured pork about 2 inches long by ¼ inch wide and thick. All of the recipes in this book call for lardons cut from slab bacon, which is ideal, but thick-cut sliced bacon will also work fine, though it may be slightly thinner than the ¼ inch thickness called for. Quality counts, so purchase organic, uncured bacon made with as few ingredients as possible. If you can find unsmoked bacon, all the better—it is traditional, though smoked bacon is acceptable in these recipes. Small-batch bacon is usually the best choice and is most easily found in butcher shops or from superior online retailers, such as Benton's Smoky Mountain Country Hams. If you can find only ordinary commercial bacon, select the brand with the most thickly cut slices and the fewest additives, such as sodium phosphates and nitrates or nitrites; thinly sliced bacon won't produce properly sized lardons. Quality slab bacon tends to not keep as long as bacon with additives, so here's a tip: freeze 2-inch cubes of slab bacon in a ziplock bag. Then, whenever you need to cut some lardons, allow the cubes to soften slightly at room temperature before slicing them the proper size.

Baguette Purchase baguettes baked as recently as possible from a quality local bakery. The crust of a baguette should be amber. When gently squeezed, it should yield slightly without being squishy and it should crackle, indicating crispness. The loaf can be eaten as is or crisped in a 350°F oven. You can do as the French often do and put it directly on the table to be torn by hand by the individual diners, or you can cut it into ½-inch-thick slices (on the diagonal if you're so inclined) and serve it in a cloth-lined basket. Always accompany it with room-temperature butter, salted or unsalted. A baguette is best eaten the day it is purchased; if you need to store it, you can place it in a large plastic bag, making sure it is well sealed. Depending on its degree of staleness, you can revive day-old baguette by lightly dampening the crust with a little water and then heating it in the oven as directed above. You can also use it to make Real French Toast (page 162). (For a guide to baguette types, see page 152.)

Beef and Veal In buying beef for these recipes, use the cut specified. Grass-fed organic beef is always preferable. Veal is the meat of calves that in the United States are between sixteen and eighteen weeks old, ideally weighing no more than 450 pounds. It is a lean meat with a clean, delicate, and slightly sweet flavor that, when of good quality and cooked correctly, is one of the world's most delicious meats. Quality raw veal is pale pink and uniform in color; purchase it at your favorite butcher or through a reliable online source such as dartagnan.com.

Butter is the most beloved cooking fat of France. For most of the recipes in this book, any good-quality unsalted butter will do, but European (or European-style) butter is the best choice because its higher butterfat content (around 82 percent or more) gives it a faster melt and silkier texture, resulting in dishes that taste better and have a better texture. Widely available brands include Lurpak, which is imported from Denmark, France's Président, Ireland's Kerrygold, as well as Plugrá, Organic Valley, and Vermont Creamery—the latter three are produced in the United States.

In baking recipes, however, where butter is a crucial component—particularly French Puff Pastry (page 194)—you must use an unsalted European butter to yield the correct results.

Chicken is of the best quality when it is labeled organic and free-range. While you can use pre-cut chicken parts for a dish like Chicken Braised in Red Wine with Mushrooms (page 132), it will taste better (and more French) if you start with a small whole bird and cut it up into pieces. Look for flesh that is plump, with moist, clear skin that gives off little aroma. A number of the recipes in this book call for chicken broth. Here is a basic French method for preparing it.

French Chicken Broth
Bouillon de Volaille

Makes about 8 cups

    2½ to 3 pounds bone-in, skin-on chicken parts (preferably dark meat)
    Bouquet garni (1 bay leaf, 3 fresh or dried thyme sprigs, 3 fresh flat-leaf parsley sprigs)
    2 celery stalks, halved crosswise
    1 carrot, peeled and halved crosswise
    1 medium yellow onion, quartered
    1 small leek, white part only, halved lengthwise
    5 white or black peppercorns
    12 cups water
    Salt

1 In a stockpot, combine the chicken, bouquet garni, celery, carrot, onion, leek, peppercorns, and water and bring to a boil over high heat. Turn down the heat to medium-low, adjusting it as needed to achieve a steady, gentle simmer, and then, using a large slotted spoon or skimmer, skim off and discard any foam that forms. Simmer slowly uncovered or with a lid placed ajar, stirring occasionally and, if desired, periodically skimming off the fat, until you have a richly flavorful broth, 3 to 4 hours. Taste the broth periodically as it cooks to observe how its flavor gradually intensifies.

2 When the broth is ready, season it with salt. Scoop out and discard the larger solids, then strain the broth through a large fine-mesh sieve into a bowl and discard all the solids in the sieve. Let cool. Store the broth in one or more airtight containers in the refrigerator for up to a week or in the freezer for up to a few months. For convenience, measure the broth by cups and store in small containers or ziplock bags so you can thaw only what you need.

Cooking Equipment What follows is not a list for a complete *batterie de cuisine*—the tools called for in a professional French kitchen—but rather suggestions for standout pieces of equipment that will make the preparation of the recipes in this book easier and more of a pleasure.

Bowls ② The most useful quality for a good mixing bowl is that it be sturdy. The material can be ceramic, glass, or metal (an unlined copper bowl, traditional for whipping egg whites, is shown). You'll need a couple of bowls in each of the standard sizes: small, medium, and large.

Cutting Board ⑤ Indispensable for prepping ingredients, of course, but for the French, an old-fashioned wooden cutting board doubles as a serving tray for appetizers, especially cheeses and charcuterie. It can range in quality from the plastic budget version, which is serviceable but prone to warping, to one made of hardwood, which is an excellent investment.

Dutch Oven ⑨ Known as a *cocotte* in the French kitchen, a Dutch oven is a must for slow-cooked braises and stews. Dutch ovens do not come in a standard size or shape—the name merely refers to a heavier-than-average pot fitted with a lid. For these recipes you'll need one that is 4 to 5 quarts, either round or oval, and with sides that are not so high that they prohibit evaporation when reducing liquid, such as is called for in Burgundy-Style Beef Braised in Red Wine (page 116). Le Creuset ⑬ is one of the finest of brands, but any good, sturdy Dutch oven will suffice. Keep in mind your dishes will have a subtly metallic taste if you're cooking foods that contain an excess of acidic ingredients (wine, lemon juice, vinegar, tomatoes) in a cast-iron pot that isn't lined with enamel.

Food Processor (not shown) This efficient, powerful tool makes quick work of grinding meat for Country-Style Pork Terrine (page 43).

Handheld Mixer (not shown) Recipes that call for an extended beating time, such as the Grand Marnier Soufflé (page 181), or for mixing up a soft dough, such as Parisian Black-and-White Cookies (page 177), come together more quickly and with less arm exhaustion with this modestly priced, lightweight tool. Do your research and invest in a quality one.

Pâté Terrine ① An oval or rectangular ceramic or metal mold, the pâté terrine is specifically designed for making terrines (some models come with a weighted press to compress the meat after the terrine is baked). Look for a pâté terrine at a specialty kitchen supply shop or an antique store that carries used kitchenware. To make the terrine

on page 43, you will need an 8½ by 4½-inch pâté terrine (though a loaf pan of the same size will also work).

Pepper Mills ④ Ground black pepper is ubiquitous in French cooking, but because some recipes call for white pepper, you would do well to have a dedicated mill for each type of pepper. Quality pepper mills, such as the French-made Peugeot models shown on page 190, are an invaluable kitchen accessory.

Pie Plate (not shown) Both the quiche on page 135 and the spinach tart on page 65 are baked in a 9½-inch pie plate, though the quiche can also be made in a tart pan (see below). The French traditionally use sturdy ceramic pie plates, though a glass or porcelain plate can also be used.

Salad Bowl ⑧ Like the cutting board, the salad bowl favored by the French is made of wood. It can be seasoned periodically by rubbing the interior with a garlic clove, which will impart a subtle garlicky note to your salad. Even the least expensive version will suffice, but a quality hardwood salad bowl, well cared for, will provide pleasure and utility for decades.

Saucepans ⑦ Stainless steel–lined copper saucepans are the finest, but a stainless-steel or even a nonstick pan will work as long as it has a heavy bottom. You'll need at least two sizes of saucepans, a small one that holds about 1½ quarts and one that holds about 2½ quarts; a larger one that holds about 3 or 4 quarts can come in handy. A saucepan with a pouring lip, as shown in ③, is handy but not necessary.

Skillet ⑩ As with the saucepans, a skillet made from nearly any material, from stainless steel to enameled cast iron to nonstick, will work as long as the pan is about 12 inches in diameter. Avoid unlined cast iron or copper, which will react with acidic foods.

Stand Mixer (not shown) A great help when making Marshmallows (page 176) and *pâte à choux* dough (see page 158), the stand mixer not only does nearly all the work but also leaves one's hands free to attend to other culinary needs.

Tart Pan (not shown) A metal tart pan with fluted or plain sides and a removable bottom is essential for making the Home-Style Rhubarb Tart on page 176. Look for one 11 inches in diameter and 1⅛ inches deep. The quiche on page 135 calls for either a pie plate (see above) or an 11-inch tart pan with a solid bottom.

Thermometer (not shown) Although not essential, an instant-read thermometer for testing the doneness of meats and poultry helps to ensure

a good result. In contrast, a candy thermometer is indispensable for testing the sugar syrup for making Marshmallows (page 176). The latter also doubles as a deep-fry thermometer, which is handy for testing the oil for french fries (page 126).

Whisk ⑥ A fundamental tool of French cooking, the whisk is put to work on vinaigrettes and sauces, custards and egg whites. Almost any whisk will do, but a well-built medium-size whisk, with sturdy looped metal wires attached to a solid wood or metal handle, will last longer and whip faster and more reliably than its less-well-made counterparts.

Cream Heavy cream, also known as heavy whipping cream, has a milk-fat content between 36 and 40 percent and will double in volume when whipped. Cream keeps longer than milk, but always sniff and taste for freshness before using.

Crème Fraîche A French sour cream–like cultured milk product with a high milk-fat content, crème fraîche is rich, thick, silky, slighty tangy, and luxuriously creamy. It is available at quality supermarkets and specialty food shops. You can substitute a high-quality *crema mexicana*, or you can thin full-fat natural sour cream with water (a few teaspoons water per ¼ cup sour cream) until it is the consistency of thick yogurt.

Dijon Mustard The mustard called for in these recipes is of the Dijon variety, a piquant condiment of mustard seeds, vinegar, and wine traditionally made in the French city of Dijon. With a powerful yet delicate and complex flavor, it's the ideal accompaniment to French-style roast meats and charcuterie. The widely available brands Grey Poupon and Maille are good, but if you can find small-batch Dijon mustard, French made or otherwise, use it. Do not use whole-grain Dijon mustard or any type that has been flavored with additional ingredients (such as tarragon or honey) for these recipes. Once opened, Dijon mustard keeps for at least 6 months in the refrigerator.

Duck Widely available at supermarkets, butchers, and Asian grocers, duck is sold both whole and also often as parts, including whole legs (called for in Duck Confit on page 118) and breasts. The skin should be a healthy pinkish yellow with no greenish tinge.

Fat and Lard The recipe for Country-Style Pork Terrine (page 42) calls for pork or beef fat, which most butchers will have on hand or by special order. Duck confit is traditionally made with rendered duck fat, which can be difficult to procure and is costly in the quantity needed, so pork lard, which is more widely available and less expensive, is listed as an ingredient in the Duck Confit recipe on page 118. You can get it from a butcher shop or, in a pinch, purchase Armour brand from a supermarket.

Fish and Mussels For Herb-Poached Fish with Beurre Blanc Sauce (page 88), use fillets of any firm white fish—whatever is freshest at the market—such as cod, grouper, or hake. For West African Rice with Fish and Vegetables (page 90), a whole red snapper or grouper works well. Fish should look firm and moist and have no fishy smell or signs of discoloration. When selecting a whole fish, choose one with bright eyes, red gills, and a glossy appearance. Always cook fish the same day you buy it.

Cured Anchovies For the purest flavor, use anchovies packed in coarse salt, which are often available at Italian, Greek, North African, and Spanish grocers. Rinse off the salt and fillet them as you would sardines (see below), though you can eat the tiniest bones. If the fillets taste too salty to you, cover them with water or milk and let soak for 15 minutes. Anchovies in salt keep indefinitely. High-quality jarred or tinned anchovies packed in pure olive oil can be substituted; store leftovers in a tightly capped glass jar in the refrigerator for up to a month.

Mussels Fresh mussels are decidedly preferred over frozen. Discard mussels that are oversized or have broken or show partly open shells. Before cooking, scrub them well with a kitchen brush and cold water and pull off any beards. (Most farm-raised mussels are sold with their beard removed, but always check for stubborn strands.)

Sardines You can use either fresh or frozen sardines for the quick-cured fillets recipe on page 86. If using frozen fish, be sure to let the fish thaw completely in the refrigerator before filleting. To fillet each fish, grip the top of the fish and, with a very sharp knife, cut along the spine from the head to the very tip of the tail, keeping the cut as close to the spine as possible. Repeat on the other side. Discard the head, spine, and tail. Then, using tweezers, carefully examine each fillet and remove any errant bones, leaving the skin intact. Finally, rinse the fillets under cool running water and pat dry.

Flour From spaetzle (page 136) to soufflé (page 181), in dough or as thickener, the flour to use is an unbleached all-purpose flour with a high protein content (between 10 to 13 percent) and no additives. King Arthur and Heckers are two excellent brands available at most supermarkets. Store flour in an airtight container in a cool, dark place. Test your flour's freshness before using by smelling it—its aroma should be benign and faintly sweet.

Harissa A North African condiment popular in Paris, harissa is made primarily of piquant red chiles and usually contains olive oil and garlic. Recipes vary, but the basic flavor is tangy, spicy, and smoky. It can be eaten with any number of dishes, including the Tunisian Salad on page 39. Harissa is available in jars at shops selling Middle Eastern and North African goods and in general supermarkets that stock a wide range of imported condiments. Once opened, harissa keeps refrigerated for up to a few months.

Herbs Many of the recipes in this book call for the addition of herbs; luckily, all of them are widely available. Seek out the best-quality specimens, and with the exception of bay leaf, oregano, and thyme, generally use only fresh herbs, not dried. Look for bright-colored, healthy-looking herbs, passing up any that show signs of yellowing or limpness. They are at their best on the day of purchase. To store, wrap in a paper or cloth towel to absorb excess moisture, then seal in a plastic bag in the refrigerator. Store dried herbs in tightly capped glass jars in a cool, dark place.

Bay Leaf ③ The eucalyptus-like aroma of bay especially enhances stews and soups. It comes in a variety of botanical types, but the most common is Mediterranean (aka Turkish or sweet) bay. Buy leaves fresh if you can, but if not, dried bay leaves are fine.

Bouquet Garni ⑤ A small bundle of herbs tied together with kitchen twine (made of pure cotton, available in hardware stores, cooking-supply stores, and many supermarkets), bouquet garni varies according to the dish. It is typically added at or near the beginning of cooking and then removed at the end before serving. There is no standard recipe, but most bundles include bay leaf, parsley, and thyme; precise quantities are given in individual recipes.

Chive ② A long, grasslike blade with a scallion-like flavor, the chive is central to Parisian cuisine, where it often appears as a garnish. You can chop or snip leftover chives (discarding any blades that have turned yellow) and use them as a topping for potatoes or eggs or toss them with abandon into a green salad.

Parsley ⑥ Appreciated for its foresty taste and deep green color, parsley is popular as both an ingredient and a garnish. Use flat-leaf parsley—also known as Italian parsley—for the best flavor. Leftover parsley can be chopped and added to salads or used as a garnish for virtually any savory dish.

Rosemary ① The piney flavor of fresh or dried rosemary complements roast meats and flavors the butter that accompanies the pan-grilled steak on page 126. The sprigs, with their thick, woody stems and dark-green needles, resemble the leaves of pine trees. Look for fressh rosemary with a deep, healthy color and no signs of dried-out or black needles.

Tarragon ④ One of the core flavors of French cuisine, tarragon has tender, slim leaves and a subtle anise-like scent and, as such, the relatively tasteless dried version does not make an acceptable substitute. A heaping tablespoon of snipped tarragon makes a lettuce salad sublime.

Thyme ⑦ The autumnal flavor of thyme lingers just under the surface of many of the recipes in this book. When mature, it has thin, woody stems and tiny, fragrant green leaves. The best is fresh; second best is dried thyme that is still on the stem, which you might come across at a farmers' market or a produce stand (or hang-dry fresh thyme sprigs in an airy, dry place for a week or two). But even store-bought dried thyme leaves will work; follow the given amount if substituting it for the fresh thyme in recipes as it can easily overpower a dish.

Lamb As with beef, be sure to use the precise cuts of lamb called for in recipes. Good lamb can be found at butcher shops, farmers' markets, and farm stands; even many ordinary grocery stores often carry New Zealand lamb, which is of excellent quality.

Lentils To make the lentil salad on page 39, you'll want lentils about half the size of common North American lentils (you can substitute the larger, more typically found variety, but you'll have to cook them longer, and their texture will not be as firm). Look for the French Le Puy variety, which are dark green and have a bright, peppery flavor, at well-stocked supermarkets or specialty food stores.

Oils Many of these recipes call for a light-colored oil with a mild flavor and a high smoke point. The workaday cooking oils of traditional Parisian cooking are peanut, sunflower, safflower, and canola. All of these are acceptable; be sure the one you use is minimally refined, which signals high quality. For recipes that call for olive oil, use a good-quality extra-virgin olive oil with a deep, fruity taste. Some recipes call for walnut oil or hazelnut oil; these are also excellent in salad dressings, mayonnaise, or other uncooked preparations. No matter the kind, oil should smell fresh and clean; discard oil with even the slightest hint of a rancid smell. Store according to expiration dates or for up to a few months in a cool, dark place (nut oils should generally be refrigerated, as they go rancid more quickly than non-nut oils).

Olives When serving olives in an *apéro*, experiment with varieties you particularly like, from brine cured to vinegar cured and everything in between. Bear in mind, however, that those that come in jars are pasteurized, which diminishes their flavor and, depending on type, crispness. More desirable are the versions that come from an olive bar at your market, and best of all are those that come in bulk from a Greek, Middle Eastern, or North African grocer—these are often unpasteurized and thus better tasting. For most of these recipes, two types of olives are suggested: Picholine, a crunchy, smallish, torpedo-shaped green olive with a tart, nutty flavor, and Niçoise, a small purple-brown olive with a faintly herbal, licorice fragrance. You can embellish the taste of olives before serving them as an appetizer with a drizzle of olive oil and a few slivers of lemon peel.

Paris-Style Ham Known in French as *jambon de Paris*, this unsmoked, poached, boneless ham is essential for a true French ham and butter sandwich (page 162). While its first recorded mention appears in 1793, the ham's traditional preparation likely goes back as far as the occupation of what is now Paris by the Celts, which dates to the third century BCE. Sometimes establishments offering good charcuterie have authentic *jambon de Paris*; online retailers also carry it. Once it is sliced, store it, tightly wrapped in plastic wrap, in the coldest part of the refrigerator for no more than a few days.

Pastry Dough To get the best results with the following three dough recipes, *pâte brisée*, *pâte sablée*, and *pâte feuilletée*, you'll need to follow the instructions to the letter—measurements, ingredients, and temperatures should not be modified. Be sure to keep the doughs cool before you bake them, and keep in mind that the raw dough will often have visible lumps of butter or shortening (this is what creates the flakiness). If a dough is too loose or soft to work with, refrigerate it for at least 15 minutes, which will stiffen it and make it easier to manipulate. Before lifting a thinly rolled-out tart dough to transfer it into a pan, slide an offset spatula under it to be sure the center isn't stuck to the work surface. When using **store-bought puff pastry**, look for a brand made with all butter, such as Dufour, which will have a better flavor and consistency than one made with vegetable shortening. Most commercial dough is sold frozen, so thaw it in the refrigerator the day before you plan to use it.

Flaky Tart Pastry

Pâte Brisée

This dough is used for the quiche on page 135 and the spinach tart on page 65; it becomes light and flaky when it bakes, transforming into the gold standard of crust. The teaspoon of sugar encourages it to brown without adding a sweet flavor. If using your fingers to mix the dough—the ideal method—move swiftly so you don't impart excessive warmth to the butter and shortening.

Makes 2 disks
- 2½ cups all-purpose flour
- 1 teaspoon sugar
- Heaping ½ teaspoon salt
- 1 cup (2 sticks) cold unsalted butter, cut into ½-inch pieces
- 4 tablespoons cold solid vegetable shortening
- ½ cup plus 1 tablespoon ice-cold water, plus more if needed

1 In a large bowl, whisk together the flour, sugar, and salt. Scatter the butter pieces over the top, then, using your fingertips or a pastry blender, mix briefly until evenly combined. Add the shortening and continue working the mixture with your fingers or a pastry blender until it feels powdery, dry, and soft, and some pea-size pieces of butter and shortening are visible. Drizzle in the water and, using a rubber spatula, stir and toss the mixture until it is dry and coarse and begins to form small balls that stick together slightly. If the dough does not stick together, add another 1 or 2 tablespoons water.

2 Working quickly, gently gather the dough together into a rough mass. Transfer the dough to a lightly floured work surface, press together gently, and then divide in half. With your fingers, press each half into a round, smooth disk about 6 inches in diameter. Wrap each disk very tightly in plastic wrap. Refrigerate for at least 1 hour before using, though overnight is best. It will keep refrigerated for up to a week.

Shortbread-Style Pastry

Pâte Sablée

This classic French pastry dough is the perfect foundation for a fruit tart, such as the Home-Style Rhubarb Tart on page 176.

Makes 1 disk
- ¾ cup (1½ sticks) plus 1 tablespoon cold unsalted butter
- 2 cups all-purpose flour

- ½ cup sugar
- Salt
- 1 egg yolk, lightly beaten

1 Cut the butter into ½-inch pieces and let it sit out until pliable but not soft. Meanwhile, in a medium bowl, whisk together the flour, sugar, and a pinch of salt. Add the butter and the egg yolk. Using your fingers, combine all of the ingredients with a rubbing motion until all are evenly mixed and you have a mixture the texture of coarse sand.

2 Working quickly, gently gather the dough together into a ball, wrap it in plastic wrap, and flatten slightly into a 1-inch-thick smooth disk. Refrigerate for at least 30 minutes before using; the dough should be cool but not so cold that it won't be pliable. It will keep refrigerated for up to a week.

French Puff Pastry

Pâte Feuilletée

This dough comes out stupendously flaky, with golden, frizzled edges that contrast with the moister, chewier layers toward its center. In folding the dough over and over, you're distributing the fat evenly so that it releases steam as it cooks, encouraging thin, crisp, separate layers to form. In the recipes in this book this dough is called for in Puff Pastry Cups with Chicken and Mushrooms (page 35), Puff Pastry with Salt-Packed Anchovies (page 157), and Puff Pastry with Strawberries and Vanilla Custard (page 158). Puff pastry dough (which originated in Hungary and Austria) can be made ahead of time and stored tightly wrapped in multiple layers of plastic wrap followed by a ziploc bag in the refrigerator for up to 3 days or in the freezer for up to 1 month. Once cooked, however, puff pastry is best eaten the same day.

Makes 2½ pounds

DOUGH A
- ¾ cup plus 3 tablespoons water, plus more if needed, at room temperature
- 1½ teaspoons salt
- 3 cups all-purpose flour, sifted

DOUGH B
- 1⅔ cups unsalted European or European-style butter, at room temperature
- ½ cup all-purpose flour, sifted

1 To make dough A, in a medium bowl, combine the water and salt and stir to dissolve the salt. Add the flour and stir using your hands or a spoon until the ingredients are well combined; if there's a lot of loose, unincorporated flour after mixing, you can add more water, 1 teaspoon at a time, not exceeding more than a few teaspoons. With your hands, form the dough into a ball, being careful not to overwork it. Wrap the ball in plastic wrap and let it rest at room temperature for 30 minutes.

2 To make dough B, be sure the butter is at room temperature; if it is too warm, the dough will be difficult to work with. In a medium bowl, combine the butter and flour with a wooden spoon and stir until well blended and a dough has formed. Place a sheet of plastic wrap on a flat work surface, transfer the dough to the plastic wrap, and use your fingers to shape and flatten it into a 6-inch square. Cover the dough square with the plastic wrap and leave it in the coldest part of the refrigerator for 20 minutes.

3 To prevent the dough from sticking, keep your work surface lightly floured throughout the following steps, brushing any excess flour off the dough before folding it. Unwrap both doughs. With a rolling pin, roll out dough A into a 12-inch square. Position it so it is a rhombus. Place the dough B square in the center of the rhombus, then fold the four corners of the rhombus over dough B, enclosing the square in an "envelope" of dough. Being sure not to overwork the dough (which would cause it to get too soft to work with), roll it out into a 6 by 16-inch rectangle, making sure to carefully press out any visible air bubbles that form. (If holes form in the dough as you roll, patch them with a pinch of flour and continue.) Orient the rectangle horizontally, then fold the left side one-third of the way toward the center, followed by the right side, making a brochure-style fold. Roll out the dough again into a 6 by 16-inch rectangle; make sure to carefully press out any visible air bubbles that form. Once more, orient the rectangle horizontally, then fold the left side one-third of the way toward the center, followed by the right side, making a brochure-style fold. Wrap the dough in plastic wrap and refrigerate it for 30 minutes.

4 Clean the work surface and then lightly flour it again. Unwrap the dough and roll it out into a 6 by 16-inch rectangle; make sure to carefully press out any visible air bubbles that form. Orient the rectangle horizontally, then fold the left side one-third of the way toward the center, followed by the right side, making a brochure-style fold. Wrap the dough tightly in multiple layers of plastic wrap and refrigerate it at least 30 minutes or until ready to use.

Preserved Lemon Called for in Tunisian Salad (page 39), Salt-Roasted Pork with Preserved Lemon and Ginger (page 123), and Lamb Tagine with Saffron and Olives (page 123), lemons preserved in salt are a delicious, tangy ingredient of North Africa. You can find jarred versions at supermarkets that stock a wide array of condiments or in shops that sell Middle Eastern or North African foods, but making your own is easy and yields a brighter flavor than store-bought.

North African–Style Preserved Lemon
Citron Confit

Makes 1 preserved lemon
> **1 medium regular or Meyer lemon, thoroughly washed, thickly sliced crosswise, and seeds removed**
> **2 tablespoons salt**

1 In a small glass jar, combine the lemon slices and salt, coating the slices evenly with the salt. Cap the jar and set aside in a warm place for 24 to 48 hours to cure.

2 To use the lemon, rinse off the excess salt with cool water and cut as directed in individual recipes. Store unused lemon in the glass jar for up to a week.

Rabbit Popular in France on both restaurant menus and in home kitchens, rabbit is a delicate, smooth-textured, lean white meat. Look for it at a good butcher shop, the meat department of a well-stocked supermarket, or online from a trusted vendor of game, such as dartagnan.com. Make sure the meat is pale pink and glossy, and if you are not ordering it online, ask the butcher to cut it up into four legs and two sections of loin. It makes a marvelous broth, too; just substitute it for the chicken in the broth recipe on page 188.

Roasting When roasting meat, consider using a thermometer to test the oven temperature, as the temperature gauge of an oven is not always accurate. Note, too, that the shallower a roasting pan is, the faster any moisture in the meat or liquid in the pan will evaporate, and the browner a roast will get. A shallow pan yields a particularly good result for roast chicken. Always position the oven rack you will be using in the middle of the oven, and place the pan in the center of the rack.

Salt In general, you should use the salt you like, except for in the recipe for pork roasted in a salt crust on page 123, which calls for medium-coarse salt, and the recipe for quick-cured sardines on page 86, which calls for coarse salt. Whatever salt

you select, it should be neither too fine nor too coarse, however, so it will melt and integrate well. A good all-purpose choice is kosher salt; Diamond, Morton, and Martin are three reputable brands. You can experiment with more exotic salts, in particular French ones, but you need to be mindful of their grind. *Fleur de sel*, for example, a French sea salt, is fine for *Ultimate Pan-Grilled Steak and Twice-Cooked Fries* (page 126), but its large crystals won't melt properly in a baking recipe. The key to getting saltiness right is to taste a dish as it cooks and to add salt along the way, allowing time for any salt you add to incorporate fully before you taste and season again. All of the recipes in this book were developed using a light hand with salt, so you should increase the amount as desired.

Sauces French sauces are among the best in the world, but many are famously difficult to salvage once they go wrong. A confidence-inspiring place to begin is with béchamel, which is called for in the spinach tart on page 65 but is also an excellent sauce to ladle warm over blanched cauliflower or broccoli.

Béchamel Sauce

This easy sauce can also be used as a base for creamed spinach, lasagna, moussaka, or even macaroni and cheese.

Makes about 1 cup
1¼ cups whole milk
Freshly grated nutmeg
2 tablespoons unsalted butter
2 tablespoons all-purpose flour
Salt and freshly ground white pepper

1 In a saucepan large enough to hold the milk, combine the milk and a pinch of nutmeg and bring to a simmer over very low heat. Simmer gently, stirring occasionally, for 1 minute, then remove from the heat.

2 In a saucepan of the same size, melt the butter over low heat. Stir in the flour, raise the heat to medium-low, and cook, stirring constantly with a wooden spoon, until the flour smells fragrant but is not yet darkening, about 3 minutes. Remove the pan from the heat, let the butter mixture cool slightly, and then slowly whisk the warmed milk into the butter-flour mixture until it is fully incorporated.

3 Return the pan to low heat and bring the mixture to a very gentle simmer, whisking continuously to prevent any lumps from forming. Taking care the mixture does not boil, cook the mixture, whisking occasionally, until it is the consistency of a thick cream-based soup, about 10 minutes. Season with salt and pepper.

Vegetables Be attuned to seasonal availability when purchasing vegetables for the recipes in this book—and strive to acquire your produce from a wholesome source, such as your nearest farmers' market.

Artichoke ⑤ Select specimens that feel heavy for their size and have tightly closed bracts, the leaflike "petals" that surround the larger bud. If using regularly sized artichokes, prepare them by removing the tough lower bracts and using scissors to snip the sharp spines off the tips of the remaining ones. **Baby artichokes** are the diminutive, low-sprouting bulbs of regular-size artichoke plants and weigh about 3 ounces each. They are too small to have developed a choke; clean them by removing their outer layer of bracts and sharp tips. Store both varieties of artichokes in a plastic bag in the refrigerator for up to a few days.

Asparagus Most asparagus spears are about a foot long and as thick as a pencil, though thickness varies. With an earthy taste and a crisp, pleasingly fibrous texture, asparagus is grown year-round but is a special treat in late spring. Before cooking, break off the pale, woody ends and discard. Be sure not to overcook the spears (the more slender they are, the faster they will cook). Asparagus is best eaten within 48 hours of purchase. **White asparagus**, called for in the asparagus soup on page 36 and in the duck confit salad on page 34, is ordinary asparagus that has been deprived of sunlight, which prevents the spears from producing chlorophyll. It has the same flavor as green asparagus and an appealing ivory color. If white asparagus cannot be found, green asparagus can be substituted.

Carrot ② Use the youngest and freshest carrots you can find, passing up woody, older specimens. Store in a plastic bag in the crisper of the refrigerator for up to a week or two.

Cassava Also known as yuca or manioc, cassava is used in the West African fish stew on page 90. A long tuber with a bark-like brown skin, it has a mild, nutty flavor, a starchy potato-like texture, and must always be peeled and cooked before eating. Look for it in African, Caribbean, and Latin American markets. To prepare cassava, cut off the ends, slice it crosswise into segments, remove the thin core that runs down the center, and use a sharp knife to peel away the skin. Store uncut cassava in the refrigerator for up to a week, or freeze peeled raw chunks in zip-tight bags for up to a few months.

Fava Beans Fresh fava beans come in large (about 6-inch-long) pods with spongy interiors; the pods are discarded, revealing a green fava bean with a thin, edible skin that should be removed for Poached Spring Vegetables with Lemongrass-Dill Dressing (page 64). Fresh fava beans are typically not easy to find (farmers' markets are your best bet), but if you do encounter them, look for younger ones, with pods about 4 inches long. Store in a plastic bag in the refrigerator for no more than a few days.

French Breakfast Radish Hot, crisp, and sweet, French breakfast radishes have a more cylindrical shape and paler color than the typical American radish. A classic Parisian way to eat them is atop a baguette slice with butter and a sprinkle of fleur de sel. Ordinary radishes may be substituted in most cases, but the French breakfast radish is de rigueur at an *apéro*. To store, remove the greens, rinse, immerse in a bowl of water, and refrigerate for a few days, changing the water daily.

Haricot Vert Also known as French beans, haricots verts are a type of green bean (or string bean) that is slimmer, shorter (about 4 inches long), and more tender than the variety most commonly found in American supermarkets. If you can't find them, use the thinnest, youngest green beans available, bearing in mind that they may take slightly longer to cook. Before cooking, trim both ends of each bean. Store in a plastic bag in the refrigerator for no more than a few days.

Potato With the exception of three recipes that call for russets, you'll get uniformly excellent results for the dishes in this book with the Yukon gold ③, a yellow-skinned potato with a creamy white interior. For New Potatoes Baked in Cream (page 64), other good options are Carola ⑦, a small, oblong variety that usually has yellow skin and sweetish yellow flesh; fingerling ①; or Red Bliss ④. No matter the variety, select firm potatoes with taut skin and no green tinge or sprouting eyes.

Shallot ⑥ With its sharp, sweet onion flavor, the French red shallot—a narrow miniature onion with coppery pink skin—is a signature ingredient of France. Other varieties of shallots are available, including the stubbier, rounder species found at Asian groceries, but using their French-species counterpart will yield the best results in these recipes. Select the smallest, firmest specimens and store them as you do onions, in a cool, dark place with good air circulation.

Vinegar Used since ancient times in French cooking, vinegar is an important note in recipes such as Herb-Poached Fish with Beurre Blanc Sauce (page 88) and, it will make or break a vinaigrette (page 57). Invest in a quality wine vinegar, preferably a small-batch or imported French brand, as a mediocre commercial supermarket brand can make a dish come out aggressively sour. You can find finer wine vinegars at specialty food shops, high-end supermarkets, and online retailers. Failing that, look for vinegars—both white wine and red wine—with no flavorings (such as garlic or herbs). Vinegar will keep indefinitely in a cool, dark place.

Wines and Liqueurs Even if a recipe calls for only a small amount of wine or liqueur, quality is of paramount importance. If you skimp by using "cooking wine" or low-quality wine, you risk throwing off the flavor of the dish. Always taste a wine before you cook with it: a good drinking wine makes for a good cooking wine. The same advice goes for liqueurs, which can also vary in quality according to their ingredients and distilling process.

WORLD FOOD

Editor and Author James Oseland
Creative Director Dave Weaver
World Food Test Kitchen Director Brenda Nieto
Kitchen Assistants Nora Bergen, Esther Guzman
Researchers Taylor Cannon, Pablo Orube
Paris Advisors Bénédict Beaugé, Philippe Bordaz, Jeanne Fiaux, Nicole Knaus, Jean-Bernard Magescas, Sanford McCoy, Mivsam Noiman, Ania Pamula, Léa Pernollet, Frédéric Ramade, Diane Reungsorn, Victoria Ross

Bibliography

Child, Julia; Louisette Bertholle; and Simone Beck. *Mastering the Art of French Cooking*, volumes 1 and 2. New York: Alfred A. Knopf, 1961.

David, Elizabeth. *French Provincial Cooking*. London: Penguin, 1960.

Escoffier, Auguste. *The Escoffier Cookbook: A Guide to the Fine Art of French Cuisine*. New York: Crown, 1989.

Fisher, MFK. *The Cooking of Provincial France*. New York: Time Life Books, 1968.

Gourmet, the Editors of. *Gourmet's France Cookbook*. New York: Gourmet Books, Inc., 1982.

Greenspan, Dorie. *Around My French Table: More Than 300 Recipes From My Table to Yours*. New York: Rux Martin/Houghton Mifflin Harcourt, 2010.

Lebovitz, David. *My Paris Kitchen: Recipes and Stories*. Emeryville: Ten Speed Press, 2014.

Rombauer, Irma S.; Becker, Marion Rombauer; and Becker, Ethan. *Joy of Cooking*. New York: Scribner, 1997.

Root, Waverly, and de Rochemont Richard. *Contemporary French Cooking*. New York: Random House, 1962.

Waters, Alice. *Chez Panisse Menu Cookbook*. New York: Random House, 1995.

Acknowledgments

I would particularly like to thank Jill Goodman, whose guidance, as usual, was astute; David Lebowitz for his gracious hospitality; and Maria Guarnaschelli, America's greatest cookbook editor, who gave of her wisdom even when she wasn't aware of it. I would also like to express my gratitude to Valentin Allegra; Jacques Ballard; Catherine Barnouin; Melissa Blum; Didier Bodelet; Robin Cawelti; Nzinghe Clark; Laura Cohen; Doe Coover; Pascal Decary; Jérôme Delafosse; Hugo Desnoyer; Jim Dodge; Alain Ducasse; John Fanning; Greg Ferro; Suzanne Fletcher; Marion Fourestier; Mara Goldberg; Frédéric Gorny; Gael Greene; Dorie Greenspan; Floré Guillet; Mike Hall; Jérémie Hebinger; Martha Holmberg; Audrey Janet and the École Gregoire-Ferrandi; Claire Kahn; Claude and Edmond Kahn; Fouad Kassab; Pam Kaufman; Cyriaque Kempf; Kakuna Kerina; David Lida; Christian Leblond; Caroline Lefevre; Maïna Le Marchard; Alexander Lobrano; Rita Marmor; David McAnich; Maura McGee; Julie Oseland; Alain Passard; Romain Pellas; Sofia Perez; Antoine Phillippe; Pascale Bossis; Carine Polito; Francine Prose; Jacqueline Pusch; Hannah Rahill; Camille Rankin; Alexandre Rimbaud; Axel Rodhe; Pauline Rolland; Regina Ross; Ruth Reichl: Harris Salat; Églantine Sauvage; Guy Savoy; Thierry Sayegh; Sharon Silva: Thor Stockman; the team at Ten Speed Press, including Emma Campion, Lorena Jones, Emma Rudolph, Mari Gill, Jane Chinn, Faith Hague, Zoey Brandt, David Hawk, Chloe Aryeh, and Aaron Wehner; Simon Thibault; Lisa and Sam Tosti; Sugio Yamaguchi; Deborah Zago; Yuri Zapanic; and Meg Zimbeck.

Index

Ten Speed Press and the Ten Speed Press colophon are registered
trademarks of Penguin Random House LLC.

Library of Congress Cataloging-in-Publication Data
is on file with the publisher.

Hardcover ISBN: 978-0-399-57983-7
eBook ISBN: 978-0-399-57984-4

Printed in China

Photo on page 42 is by Robert Doisneau/Gamma-Rapho via Getty Images

Designer | David Weaver
Food and prop stylist | James Oseland
Map | Mike Hall
Acquiring editor: Hannah Rahill | Editor: Emma Rudolph
Designer: Emma Campion | Production designers: Mari Gill and Faith Hague
Production manager: Jane Chinn | Prepress color manager: Nick Patton
Copyeditor: Sharon Silva | Proofreader: Rachel Markowitz
Indexer: Ken Della Penta

10 9 8 7 6 5 4 3 2 1

First Edition